OMNICIDE

OMNICIDE

The Nuclear Dilemma

LISL MARBURG GOODMAN
AND
LEE ANN HOFF

PRAEGER

New York
Westport, Connecticut
London

JX
1974.7
.G663
1990

Library of Congress Cataloging-in-Publication Data

Goodman, Lisl Marburg.
    Omnicide : the nuclear dilemma / Lisl Marburg Goodman and Lee Ann
Hoff.
        p.   cm.
    Includes bibliographical references.
    ISBN 0-275-93298-2 (alk. paper)
    1. Nuclear disarmament.   2. United States—Foreign relations—
Soviet Union.   3. Soviet Union—Foreign relations—United States.
I. Hoff, Lee Ann.   II. Title.
JX1974.7.G663   1990
303.6′6—dc20   90-31363

Library of Congress Catalog Card Number: 90-31363
ISBN: 0-275-93298-2

First published in 1990

Praeger Publishers, One Madison Avenue, New York, NY 10010
An imprint of Greenwood Publishing Group, Inc.

Printed in the United States of America

#21081109

∞™

The paper used in this book complies with the
Permanent Paper Standard issued by the National
Information Standards Organization (Z39.48–1984).

10 9 8 7 6 5 4 3 2 1

105596

To Sammy, Marie, and Frans,

and

to all those who have dedicated themselves
to saving our planet

Contents

Figures and Tables

FIGURES

TABLES

Preface

Life in the nuclear age is utterly different from any other period in human history. In the past we went through dark ages marked by pestilence, wars, genocides, and inquisitions that were interspersed with periods of peace and enlightenment; whole civilizations did rise and fall. Yet never before has the fate of our entire planet—possibly its total annihilation—been at stake.

What makes our age so unparalleled in history is that we can never again fully recuperate that time of innocence some short 50 years ago when humans did not possess the potential of destroying their own world. No matter how much progress we achieve in peace-making and peace-keeping—even if all the nuclear arsenals were destroyed—we would never be rid of the knowledge that humans could rebuild and unleash forces capable of annihilating all life on Earth.

Albert Einstein could see the abyss we were approaching head-long when he warned that "the splitting of the atom has changed everything save our mode of thinking, and thus we drift toward unparalleled catastrophe." Clearly, what needs to be changed is our way of viewing the world. In an attempt to unravel the threats that have led to the current nuclear dilemma, this book starts by exploring the need to push knowledge forward as far as humanly possible (the discovery of nuclear energy being a case in point), while remaining responsible for controlling what is done with that knowledge.

Three questions are addressed in this book. They focus on the past, the present, and the future.

1. How did we get to where we are?
2. What are the effects of the nuclear threat on our lives?
3. Where can we go from here?

In Part I, through an analysis of the outdated notion that aggression and violence are inevitable responses to human conflict, we hope to lay to rest the myth of innate aggression—which would make warfare out to be as inevitable as the tides. Our clinging to this myth has caused an abdication of responsibility, and put the fate of our planet in the hands of those few powerful individuals who try to convince us that they know better than we do. This abdication has led to feelings of powerlessness, desensitization, and passivity as well as to a denial of the nuclear threat itself—a syndrome we label here "omnicidal." Critical examination of the psychodynamic, sociocultural, and political-economic factors that wind through our lives in a complex interrelationship reveals how these factors keep us locked to a denial of reality, and consequent inaction.

This book also investigates the link between the insecurities of life in the nuclear age and the increasing rate of youth suicide, apathy, and disengagement, and the general devaluation of life without a secure future. Throughout the book, alternate ways of thinking and acting are explored—with emphasis on the change from aggressive/competitive modes to negotiation and cooperation, from feelings of helplessness to empowerment and confidence, and from apathy to action toward social change.

These theoretical analyses lay the foundation for Part II in which are presented the findings from several studies conducted with hundreds of people in North America and Europe. Our studies reveal the pervasiveness of fear, denial, a fatalistic world view, and the omnicidal personality pattern that we link to personal and social problems.

Part III presents social change strategies that can be adopted at the individual, family, and socio-political levels to promote peace. Major themes in this section include the pivotal role of child-rearing and educational approaches that emphasize cooperative behavior and critical thinking about global issues. Our attitude is one of hope in humanity's ability to turn the nuclear tide (which, after all, is a human construction), whose course we can redirect to create a safer, more humane global society.

The primary audience for this book is the educated general reader. It is also appropriate as a major resource for college students in peace studies and in the social, behavioral, and health sciences.

Omnicide differs from other works on nuclear threat in several ways. One unique feature is its blend of broad philosophical/theoretical themes and themes in the peace studies and conflict literature with the results of extensive research: we surveyed the attitudes of hundreds of adults in the United States and Europe, as well as children and youth in the United States. Our analysis links the pessimism and lack of motivation among youth and the denial of reality among adults to the conscious or unconscious fear of nuclear holocaust. The book concludes on a note of optimism, however, with visions and strategies for a lasting peace.

Acknowledgments

We wish to thank Betty Reardon and Stephen Nathanson for reading the manuscript and for their constructive criticism and warm encouragement.

Prologue

DESENSITIZATION TO NUCLEAR REALITIES

It is almost beyond comprehension how we accept the most dramatic of revelations almost instantly, with relative equanimity: our capacity to murder Earth and level it to the condition of another moon, rotating lifeless around on its axis. This devastating ability for total annihilation was not fully realized until recently. Realization came only after scientists all over the world apprised us of the consequences of exploding a large enough nuclear arsenal anywhere in the world: nuclear winter! Before that—at least since 1945—we knew of the nuclear peril in terms of unimaginable suffering, the possible death of millions of people, and primitization of the surviving. As horrifying as these prospects were, they are of a totally different dimension from the cessation of Earth as a life-sustaining planet.

Yet, the vast majority of the well over 1,000 people we surveyed go about their everyday lives seemingly without worrying too much about the nuclear threat— and that, in spite of admitting that the threat is real and that nuclear war within their lifetime is very possible. But too many other threats are felt to be more immediate and therefore demanding of greater attention. Concerned citizens have told us that we humans are already well on the way to hastening the end of our world—without a nuclear holocaust. We are destroying the Earth anyway by defoliating its forests, polluting the seas and waterways, poisoning our drinking water, depleting the ozone layer, fouling the air we breathe, and contaminating our food with pesticides.

Other dangers mentioned pertain to the unbalanced global economy: overpopulation, hunger and starvation in many parts of the world, and the lack of shelter witnessed even in the more prosperous Western world among the ever-increasing homeless individuals and families. Drug abuse and violence have reached epidemic proportions as seen in the number of rapes, acts of incest, child and wife batterings, homicides, and suicides. And the AIDS pandemic is not abating, but increasing.

However, the factor underpinning all these self-destructive phenomena is life in the nuclear age. The ravaging of the environment is a clear and telling proof of disrespect for nature and for our planet. If we do not care about safekeeping resources for our future generations, what is there to prevent us from committing any act of violence toward our Earth, as long as the act seems to bring a momentary advantage to its perpetrators? Nuclear waste, nuclear fallout, and finally nuclear devastation are certainly the ultimate in violence to our environment.

As to the world's economic woes, they too are related to the nuclear dilemma. The arms race—swallowing up 40 percent of resources worldwide—prevents us from providing adequate care to the hungry, the homeless, the sick, and the aged; it keeps us from properly educating our population and providing a balanced distribution of life-sustaining resources to our global community.

The domestic violence among us, the all-pervasive drug abuse, the escalating rate of suicides committed at younger and younger ages can also all be linked to a society in which aggression, violence, and a devaluation of life is seen as the solution to conflicts, and nuclear retaliation accepted as the final solution.

The fear of nuclear holocaust fluctuates with the slightest changes in political tension. When our leaders are hawkish—as in the recent days of "evil empire" rhetoric—then nuclear war becomes a fearful reality. But the moment there is a thaw—as in the present time of Gorbachev and the dramatic events in Eastern

Europe—the nuclear threat is perceived as irrelevant, and we seem to lose interest. It is of vital importance to realize, however, that nothing has changed as far as the danger to our planet is concerned. We still possess the potential to destroy our own country, our opponent's country, and all the countries in between within minutes—and the rest of the world within weeks. Currently there is indeed a glimmer of hope that we may find a solution to the nuclear dilemma. Maybe our world will be saved after all, at least for the foreseeable future. But we must understand that we can never go back to the age of innocence—to a pre-nuclear age. Even if we succeed in destroying all existing nuclear weapons, we still live with the threat that they can be produced again.

This seeming loss of interest in matters of war and peace at times of relative détente is of grave importance. It amounts to abdication of all responsibility, putting the fate of the Earth in the hands of a few. And actually it is not so much a lack of interest as it is a numbness to the nuclear threat.

Let us imagine the following scenario: You have just arrived in the Western world after having lived for years on a remote island in virtual isolation. Suddenly and unexpectedly you are brought up to date by a friend: A few men actually have the power at their fingertips to start the irreversible destruction of the Earth within minutes. It sounds like a science-fiction horror story. But you know that your informer is absolutely serious and most reliable and trustworthy.

Your reaction is one of acute terror: you feel nauseous; your hands tremble; your legs are shaking; you break out into a cold sweat. This is really a mild reaction to the enormity of the revelation. Yet your informer looks at you as if you were behaving most inappropriately. He thinks that the long isolation must have rendered you somewhat weird, probably in need of psychotherapy. You run out of his office and right into another colleague. Breathlessly you confront her with the news you have just received. She shrugs her shoulders, smiles a bit sadly (or is it cynically?), and says, "So what else is new?" You wonder if everyone is on drugs now. Or have they simply gone mad? Notions of a mass brainwashing or some new form of subtle hypnotism come to mind.

You confront everyone you meet with the "news" of possible world destruction, in the hope of finding at least one other soul who feels the way you do. In vain. People start whispering about you; there are intimations that your long isolation has affected your stability. Eventually you understand what has happened here: you have simply not been exposed to the gradual process of desensitization that all your friends have undergone. Nuclear realities were shrouded in secrecy, and only slowly did the most gruesome facts leak out. By the time people had the whole story—or as much of the whole story as can be known without firsthand experience of apocalypse itself—they had become numb. An enormous burden has suddenly fallen on our friend's shoulders: He must bring the world to its senses before it is too late.

BRINGING THE WORLD TO ITS SENSES

Of necessity, this book does not aim to bring the world to its senses. Indeed, the world *can* be brought to its senses—out of its psychic numbing—but only if each one of us comes to her or his senses. We cannot wait or hope for the grandiose act of one person. The responsibility for saving the world is on everyone's shoulders. No gigantic steps are needed: one small step for each human, one giant leap for all humankind. Taking even that one small step is impossible, however, so long as denial dominates our response to the threat of nuclear holocaust—denial fueled by fear. Coming up with explanations for the modern scourge of violence and aggression is not sufficient. We must lift the psychic numbing from our minds and hearts so that action can replace apathy, hope can displace despair, and a cooperative approach to life on Earth can finally eliminate the possibility of omnicide.

Our overriding concern here is this: no matter what the reasons for our present dilemma, we can no longer afford a competitive approach to interpersonal and global conflict if we would avoid the unparalleled catastrophe of global self-destruction.

I

How Did We Get to Where We Are?

1

On Human Nature and the Culture of Aggression

We are living in the nuclear age. We have discovered sources of energy that, if released in sufficient amount, can destroy our world. As awesome as this discovery may have been, we did not stop there but went on to develop technologies that put this destructive potential to practical use. Knowing the devastating consequences that the production and storage of these instantly usable nuclear weapons now have, one wonders why we proceeded as we did. Many explanations invoke human nature, and most specifically the aggressive instinct. This chapter will briefly review various arguments for how we got to where we are—not in order to settle questions that scientists and philosophers still struggle with worldwide, but to place these arguments in the context of their function in maintaining an aggressively destructive culture, a reality-denial system, and lethargy when it comes to social change.

THE GOOD/BAD ARGUMENT

Throughout the ages, philosophers have argued as to whether humans are basically good, kind, and cooperative or bad, aggressive, and competitive. Leibniz and Rousseau are the most familiar proponents of the first position; Machiavelli and Voltaire of the second. Leibniz claimed that nothing can be essentially wrong in this best of all possible worlds. Rousseau took Leibniz's claim to its logical conclusion. If all is for the best in this best of all possible worlds, how can we explain the death of thousands of people that occurred in the horrible Lisbon earthquake of November 1, 1755. The answer—Rousseau claimed—lies simply in showing that the good human nature has been interfered with by society, which has enticed these basically noble creatures—who are all part of nature—into the unnatural environment of the corrupt city, thereby stunting their natural unfolding. However, in this best of all possible worlds, the earthquake was a blessing in disguise, since it will bring the people back to nature!

Voltaire was incensed when reading Rousseau's now famous *Letter on the Earthquake in Lisbon.* Sheer brilliance and sarcasm so gushed from the critic's pen and with such speed that one of the finest gems in all literature—*Candide*—came out in just three weeks. The tale was Voltaire's answer to Leibniz and Rousseau. It makes a farce of the notions that human beings are basically good and that this is the best of all possible worlds. In any case, these two relatively short classic works—the *Letter on the Earthquake* and *Candide*—stand as thesis and antithesis to the dichotomy of good and evil in human nature. In current psychology we still find adherents to one or the other position—seeing humans as innately good or inherently evil. Carl Rogers is probably the best known advocate of the basically good person. As long as a person's growth is not interfered with by negative forces in the environment (and according to Rogers, anything short of unconditionally positive regard is negative), all will be for the best.

THE AGGRESSIVE INSTINCT AND ITS SUBLIMATION

Freud's theory of the death instinct, along with its derivatives in the destructive urges of human beings, is paradigmatic in its view of human nature as possessed innately by negative forces. The death instinct—present at birth—is opposed by the life instinct, and thus not allowed to manifest itself in its original form. But that destructive urge is there, with all its tension and struggle for release. It expresses itself—turning outward—as the aggressive instinct. And in his darkest moments, Freud sees the death instinct as condemning us forever to warfare.

Yet with all its pessimism, Freud's view of humanity is not utterly hopeless. There is more within the human potential than just blind instincts driving us forever to repeat the same pattern, and with one aim: self-destruction. Humanity is not all "id" (the Freudian storehouse where our instincts dwell), but we have (or rather, we are) "ego," the conscious part of our being—which sits in the saddle, holding the reins, planning and choosing and giving direction to our lives. True, eventually the "ego founders upon the id" (in death) as so succinctly put by Rilke; but before we succumb, there is a lifetime of becoming aware of the forces that drive us (making the unconscious conscious is, after all, the ultimate goal of Freudian psychoanalysis) and gaining the power to combat and control them and use their energy to our best advantage. Thus—according to Freud—we are capable of sublimating our aggressive instinct and channelling its energy into any direction we want it to take. This is Freud's explanation for all specifically human achievements—our most sublime acts, and our entire culture.

Does all this mean, then, that human nature is basically good, kind, and cooperative—as the self-actualization theorists maintain—leaving us at a loss to explain the nuclear dilemma, at least in terms of an innate aggressive instinct? The either/or, good/bad views of humanity are simplistic and incomplete at best. Every human being is born with a full range of human potentials. They include aggression, greed, self-interest, altruism, compassion, creativity—the list goes on and on. Why some individuals develop primarily their positive potentials, while others are beset with the most destructive human characteristics, has been debated by philosophers for centuries. Their arguments revolve around the age-old controversy of nativism versus environmentalism, or the nature/culture debate. This debate is significant not only as it concerns human beings generally, but also with respect to gender—especially in recent critiques of the social sciences.

Whether we inherit our personality characteristics or acquire them after conception is really a pseudo-problem, however. If indeed there is a gene responsible for destructiveness, the very same gene is also then the transmitter of creativeness—the opposite side of the same coin. It seems that we need to think of everything exhibited by humans as being possibilities or potentials within all of us. We differ from one another as to which of the potentials we each can or do develop.

And—in fact—in recent literature (for example, Charney 1982), we find a new version of the theory that ties aggression to heredity. Some authors assert that every human being is capable of performing the vilest, most inhumane act ever committed by any human being if such an act happens to be demanded by the present circumstances. This view has been used to explain—for example—how thousands of civilized people could have committed the enormous atrocities that occurred in Nazi Germany. According to Charney (1982), we need to become aware of the dangers that lurk within ourselves in order to fight consciously the manifestation of our most cruel and violent tendencies. Carried to its extreme, this new look in personality theories seems just as unfounded as the earlier good/bad dichotomy of human nature. No matter what the present circumstances might demand, not every one of us could rise to the self-effacing martyrdom of a hero, or develop Callas's singing voice, or put a knife into another human being. The absence of any one of these abilities or characteristics is neither virtuous nor immoral. They are simply not within everyone's repertoire of potentialities.

More than a few modern arguments have been put forth in defense of human aggression. They rest primarily on Darwinism and—more specifically—on Konrad Lorenz's bio-sociology (ethology), which emphasizes the survival value as well as the ennobling aspects of aggression. According to Lorenz, it is thanks to the aggressive instinct that the human species was able to defend itself early on against a hostile environment. It weeded out those who were least adapted for survival through natural selection, assuring perpetuation of the fittest. Aggression led to the conquest of all the Earth's habitable territory, together with dispersion of its resources. But beyond considerations of survival, Lorenz views the discharge of aggression as a virtue when it is channelled toward ethically acceptable targets, such as "militant enthusiasm."[1]

True, the aggressive drive may have been integral to survival at the dawn of human history when the most basic human needs—food, shelter, safety—could only be wrested from the raw, inhospitable environment through constant struggle, at a time before the truly human resources had a chance to develop. But even among early Hunters and Gatherers, cooperative traits were equally important and integral to survival. There may have been a time when cannibalism was considered a prerequisite for survival; head-hunting, slavery, and parricide may all have seemed to be inalienable elements of the human condition. Today we consider these practices inhuman, while excusing our own aggressive practices—from child and mate abuse, to killing each other in wars, to mass murder—as being just a part of human nature, and thus not within our power to change. We go even a step further, rationalizing that not aggression—but love—is responsible for our readiness to strike our children or to fight the enemy. Love of our country, love of God, love of freedom and liberty, all these noble sentiments are used—or rather abused—to protect us from guilt and anxiety and to maintain our present way of relating to each other.

AGGRESSION AND SEX-ROLE STEREOTYPES

The myth of "man the hunter" is another instance of claiming the existence of an innate aggressive instinct on the basis of a myth that grew out of our own constructed accounts of hunting and gathering societies. According to this myth, hunting was the primary subsistence source and was done only by the men, while the women gathered nuts and berries close to the campground. Since the hunt involved aggressive pursuit away from the settlement, and its success was a symbol of manly achievement, the image of "man the hunter" came to be associated with man's natural characteristics while "woman the gatherer" staying close to home was also construed as natural.

Today we know that gatherers also hunted and that both hunters and gatherers must have done more gathering than hunting, since most subsistence food came from gathering. And even more importantly, success in the hunt required not only aggression, but also cooperation—a fact that early descriptions of pre-state societies failed to note (Hubbard 1983: 62–63). Also, male–female relationships among groups such as the !Kung Bushmen are the most egalitarian of any society studied—a fact attributed to the equal participation of men and women in the production, distribution, and consumption of goods. Instead of using these early egalitarian societies as models of cooperation, however, theorists have imposed their own deterministic interpretation of competition and warfare on the data as justification for their arguments about innate aggression.

There is no evidence that our commitment to warfare can be blamed on an innate instinct beyond our control. We are not fated to engage forever in warfare, with total self-destruction the only release from that bondage—most of history notwithstanding. To believe that past events are the best predictors of the future is outmoded pseudo-science. On the contrary, flux and change are the only inevitabilities in all things physical and mental. There is nothing innately static about human beings or the world they inhabit. It is not within the human repertoire to go backward; the only path open is a forward one.[2] And we certainly have greater control and freedom over future events than over past ones. Freedom of choice and responsibility dwell in the future, together with all possibilities.

Even if the aggressive instinct has had a useful role in evolutionary development and adaptation, it certainly does not reign supreme. We can and very often do restrain, control, or change instinctual manifestations. There is just as much evidence to support a cooperative approach to human conflict as there is to support an aggressive one.

The glorification of aggression is also evident in a study of sex-role stereotypes conducted by Broverman and associates (1970). Not only were mental health clinicians shown to judge the common male traits of aggression and assertiveness as being characteristic of a healthy adult, but it was also evident that they tend to view the typical female traits of passivity and self-effacement as characteristics of an unhealthy adult. This study and recent reinterpretations of child-rearing patterns and sex-role stereotyping raise several pertinent questions about aggression, its origin, and the difference in its expression between men and women.

The sociobiology of aggression suggests not only that the aggressive instinct is innate, but also that it is tied to the male and female hormone systems. History seems to support this suggestion in the political arena; men have always dominated in the planning and fighting of wars. And at the interpersonal level, throughout the world wherever records are kept, the largest share of violence and aggression is carried out by men (Reardon 1985). However, the evidence of science shows no causal relationship between aggression and male hormones: not all men are aggressive, and there are some aggressive women. Thus, hormones are neither a necessary nor a sufficient cause for aggression. Furthermore, both sexes have male as well as female hormones, and both sexes may acquire violent modes of behavior from environmental influences.

Recent child-rearing studies may best account for the male/female differences evident in aggression and power relationships. Mother's primary role in parenting is a worldwide pattern of long standing, and has had a fundamental (now more or less changing) influence on the behavior and self-image of both women and men (see Chapter 9 and also Dinnerstein 1977, Chodorow 1978, Keller 1983b, Miller 1976). The disparities and similarities between men and women in leadership roles also now reveal a more complex picture of power than the simplistic either/or power differentials between men and women. In Parts II and III we elaborate further on gender differences in attitudes toward the nuclear threat.

But we still need to ask what lies behind the dominant choice of aggression over cooperation. Why do we resist changing our mode of thinking and behaving even though we know it will take us—as Einstein warned—toward "unparalleled catastrophe"? Is it the simple urge to destroy that has led to the development of more and more sophisticated, more and ever more deadly weapons to the point where we can now demolish every city in the world with more than 100,000 inhabitants eight times over? Probably not. There is no indication that any of the individuals responsible for bringing us to the brink of self-annihilation are so driven by destructive urges. They are motivated by self-interest (shortsighted as it may be), greed, and the desire for power and control. All of these traits reflect competitive (rather than cooperative) characteristics—which can lead to aggression and destruction, but are not identical with the destructive instinct that is usually blamed for the nuclear dilemma we find ourselves in.

The distinction between the aggressive instinct and competitiveness is an important one. It has been repeatedly demonstrated, in societies as well as on an individual basis, that we can abandon competitiveness for cooperation since more and more such patterns are being traced to child-rearing practices and the socialization process—not to heredity. But, as already discussed, the concept of an aggressive instinct has taken on an almost mystical connotation: we are fated to repeat forever the vicious cycle of aggressiveness. There is no choice. At the end of the path lies irrevocable self-destruction—a self-fulfilling prophecy, if ever there was one.

In the distant past, aggressiveness per se had a survival value it no longer has. But unlike other vestiges that atrophy when no longer useful, aggression is still exercised as an acceptable mode of contemporary human behavior, employed by world leaders as well as many in everyday life. Though we may observe very few spontaneous, overt aggressive actions in our everyday life, we often encounter aggression as a strategy—a way to get things done. It is regarded as a perfectly necessary tool for gaining compliance—a means of attaining or maintaining power, from the bedroom to the boardroom. All our social institutions from family to government are based on this power structure. We have only to look at any new organization being formed. Whatever the members' incipient ideology (often egalitarian), they quickly fall into the same old mold of maintaining themselves through a coercive structure that always revolves around power: buying power (that is, newly acquired economic status, whether among senior citizens or women), black power, people power, and so forth.[3] Note that each of these organizations (or movements) consists of a group that has been oppressed. Successfully shaking off oppression means to acquire and wield power. And what we also observe is that these formerly oppressed groups often repeat the same oppressive dominant behavior toward those less fortunate than themselves—those who have taken their place in the lower ranks of the hierarchy. In his *Pedagogy of the Oppressed*, Freire (1970) has brilliantly described this "oppressed group behavior." (See also Roberts 1983.)

VESTED ECONOMIC INTERESTS

However, there is another two-pronged obstacle to curbing aggressive power drives: greed and the protection of vested interests. Just as insecure people find it difficult to give up certain advantages of a dependent position, so those in power find it difficult to give up the enormous economic privileges of traditional power and control. Of all the obstacles we face, greed is probably the most insidious and the most shortsighted. In fact, the protection of vested interests may be a far greater culprit in our nuclear dilemma than the aggressive drive, whether innate or learned. When personal aggressive tendencies—coupled with people's dependence on arms production jobs for their living—are linked to the political economy and the influence of corporate profit, the enormity of our challenge in stopping the arms race is truly daunting. Whatever our position as individuals in the social structure, we have all encountered the overwhelming resistance that arises when it comes to giving up vested interests.

Similarly, candidates running for elective positions rarely run on a platform based on their convictions. Rather, they devise a platform that will have the best chance of winning the election. Similarly, officeholders tend to defend any position taken by their superiors, muting their own voices of conscience with rationalizations. Thus, Kennedy's inner circle did not see his position in the Bay of Pigs as immoral; nor did the aides involved in the Watergate and Iran–Contra scandals.

Looking at the most powerful people in the world—the heads of state actively engaged in the nuclear chess-match—we probably will not find any of them guided by an especially aggressive drive. Why then have they followed a path that insists on nuclear arsenals as an appropriate defense? We think the concept of "gamesmanship" is a better explanation for their courting of war than any specific desire to destroy the enemy. In this case, the desire to win—whatever winning may mean—takes precedence over any risks that may be involved. As a matter of fact, risk-taking seems to be the very nature of the game. The pace of the game is self-accelerating, and for once the players have not even bothered to use a euphemism. Indeed, it is a race: the arms race!

Protecting vested interests still plays the major role. This means maintaining the power, influence, and control that, in the United States, is synonymous with the interests of the most powerful group: the military–industrial complex. The major aim of industry is profit—not peace. In our present economic structure, the greatest profit is derived from government contracts—the biggest chunk of which is somewhat euphemistically called "defense." Whenever the profit motive is attacked, the counterargument always revolves around the jobs created, the standard of living we enjoy, and in general all the economic benefits we derive, thanks to big industry.

A rough estimate is that 1 percent of the employed population in the United States—or about 1 million people—are in defense-related jobs. Their vested interest in their jobs—and the threat of unemployment—is so overwhelming that we find the same process of rationalization at work in those who occupy relatively low-echelon positions as we find in top-position people. Again, it is hardly an exaggerated aggressive drive that keeps engineers in the development, refinement, and maintenance of the most lethal weapons they can possibly come up with, but rather vested personal interest and frequently greed.

In our interviews with people who work in defense, we observed that they most frequently use these four strategies in shrugging off any responsibility for engaging in potentially destructive occupations:

1. denial that what they are doing is in any way related to war and destruction;

2. flag-waving patriotism;

3. "my quitting wouldn't make any difference; someone else would get my job"; and

4. "I have no other skills; I would be unemployed."

Unfortunately, this last argument has a poignant ring of truth. For example, when the Catholic bishop in Amarillo, Texas, urged employees of the Pantex Corporation (an arms producer) to give up their jobs, he also offered employment counseling to those needing it through the local Catholic Charities organization. In response to this protest against arms production, the local United Way organization immediately cut off its grant to the Catholic Charities group. Here we have just one example of the awesome and pervasive power of the military–industrial complex.

Some of our best economists (for example, Galbraith 1981) have repeatedly indicated that our war industry could be converted into a peace industry within a matter of months, stimulating new creative directions in ideas and productivity. Yet the majority of people in fixed employment have become so security minded and fearful about any possible interference with their standard of living that possible world destruction seems easier to take than risking any of their presently enjoyed fringe benefits.4

Arguments in favor of arms production are complemented by another factor, especially in U.S. society: the deeply embedded cultural value of individual rights. In a complex relationship with the profit motive and exaltation of the competitive spirit, the individual has achieved near cult status. For example, the individual citizen's right to bear arms contributes to some extent to the U.S. record as the most violent society in the world (except for countries that are currently at war). In a society where it is easier to purchase a gun than to cash a check, where young children are fed television fare that entertains primarily by demonstrating how to blow up one's enemies, and where these practices are defended in the name of freedom of expression and the right to turn a profit, it is easy for people to rationalize the arms race as the logical extension of a socially approved climate of violence and destruction.

But regardless of how or why we got to where we are, our potential now for total destruction at the push of a button may finally function as a warning signal heard by people all over the world, and result in a new way of thinking—a new way of relating to each other. We cannot remind ourselves enough of Einstein's lucid comment: "The splitting of the atom has changed everything save our mode of thinking, and thus we drift toward unparalleled catastrophe."

2

Second Paradise Lost

THE THIRST FOR KNOWLEDGE

All of the human characteristics and needs discussed in the last chapter—aggressiveness, greed, the traditional power drive, the need to control and protect vested interests—are not solely responsible for driving us to the brink of annihilation. Strangely, it is probably the most noble, most elevating human feature—when combined with these baser motives—that also contributes to our eventual destruction: our unquenchable thirst for knowledge. Know we must—whatever the price and wherever it may take us.

The most uniquely human longing is to know the unknowable. The search for knowledge and meaning is the major theme that runs through recorded history—in myths, legends, folklore, Bible stories, the scientific enterprise, and the great tragedies of world literature. They all revolve around the drama of our insatiable need to wrench the great secret from nature; we are never fully successful in unravelling it, and always pay the price for every step we take. This secret must possess the answers to all the questions that have ever eluded us: what is the reason—or, more fundamentally, is there any reason—for our being here? Is there a beginning to space and time, and what came before the beginning? What lies beyond all existing universes, beyond space? These are the Kantian noumena—categories that philosophers have wrestled with and found to be beyond the limits of the human senses to grasp. Thus

Goethe has his Faust proclaim, "I know that we cannot know anything." (In contrast to Faust's servant, who says that he knows a great deal but wants to know everything.) Yet Faust goes on to sell his soul to the devil in exchange for youth and knowledge.

The best known example of the human need to know at any risk is contained in the oldest drama of Western civilization: the story of Adam and Eve. Eve—so it is written—was not satisfied with living happily forever after in paradise—she had to know the "secret." And according to some 500 million people, we are still being punished for Eve's acquiring of the forbidden knowledge: we are born with the original sin—the sin of losing our innocence through knowledge, of wanting to be like God. Thus, Adam and Eve became mortals, changing the order of things by giving birth to others of their kind: the human species.[1]

The same leitmotif runs through legends of the most diverse cultures. The protagonist has to know or to discover the truth, though warned implicitly or explicitly against unravelling its secret. And the search always involves a risk of losing that which is most precious to the protagonist. In Genesis there is another example of a curious woman—Lot's nameless wife—who disobeyed the divine command not to look back at the destruction of Sodom and Gomorrah. She just had to turn around and see—only to become instantly rigidified into a pillar of salt. In the German version of the legend of the Holy Grail, disaster is brought on again by an inquisitive woman. Elsa von Brabandt had been warned by Lohengrin, *"Nie sollst Du mich befragen"* ("Never shalt thou ask me"). Yet know she must; and she asks the forbidden question, only to lose Lohengrin and to die instantly herself upon learning the secret.

In contemporary reinterpretations of the Scriptures and other literature, these dramatic consequences of women's desire to know are seen as punishments, or symbolic representations of the social structure and the general constraints on women in exercising their human quest for knowledge (Okin 1979). More recent examples of the consequences inflicted on female curiosity are the proclamations of nineteenth-century physicians that the education of women would hinder them in their natural and divinely ordained destiny as producers and rearers of children (Ehrenreich and English 1979).

Yet it is not only the womenfolk who long to unravel secrets. We have already mentioned Dr. Faust. And there is also Oedipus who—fully aware that his ignorance is indeed bliss—nevertheless must learn the truth, however disastrous its consequences. Mary Shelley's original Frankenstein story—written in the early nineteenth century—provides the most fitting analogy to our present-day nuclear dilemma: how far can we go in the pursuit of scientific knowledge without the penalty of destroying ourselves in the process?

Dr. Frankenstein is driven by the ambition to learn "the secrets of heaven and earth" and is a student of alchemy, magic, and natural philosophy. He has inquired into the very "principles of life" to discover the cause of life's generation. Translated into present-day academic lingo, Frankenstein is studying chemistry, physiology, elemental physics, and genetics. Not only is he successful in discovering the stuff of which life is made, but he also acquires the technology to give life to his creation.

Originally Frankenstein's intentions are only the best. His attributes and aspirations have been described as angelic and extraordinarily gifted; even in ruin, he is a "glorious spirit" (Small 1973). Frankenstein intends his creation to be beautiful and selects its features to that end. But something goes wrong; it turns out hideous and terrifying. The monster he has created eventually turns against Frankenstein, addressing him as slave: "You are my creator, but I am your master." Here we recognize the parallel to our present condition.

The aim of science has always been to gain understanding of the laws of nature. In the noblest spirit of inquiry, our best minds have probed into the macroscopic and microscopic matters of our universe, and reported back their tentative explanations for its workings. Through this process of discovery, there emerged a certain harmless enough looking formula: $E = mc^2$ (energy equals mass times the speed of light, squared). But as one thing leads to another, this discovery soon wrenched from the atom its secret sources of energy, which if unleashed can trigger automatic chain reactions beyond our control and capable of destroying the very life of our planet.

Hardly anyone—including the scientists who made these awesome discoveries—would be willing to risk world annihilation as the price for unravelling heretofore secret aspects of nature. But neither were they ignorant of the potential consequences of their endeavors, as reflected in Einstein's statement to the effect that the creative process may very well be self-propelled: once set in motion, it cannot be stopped. And in a similar vein, Robert Oppenheimer (Moss 1968) questioned whether "the creative process can be stopped, and if so, at what point." He referred to the atomic bomb as "technically sweet" and explained that when you see something so technically sweet, you go ahead and run with it, and argue about its effects only after the technical success.

Another frequently entertained position holds that we should live like guests on this Earth, leaving it to future generations the way we found it. However, this view is a romantic distortion of reality. How did our current generation find it? Fairly hospitable, thanks to the investment of energy and resourcefulness on the part of all these past generations who worked to adapt the environment to human needs. It is to them that we owe our ever-increasing longevity, and even the survival of our species. We need not feel guilty for the changes we have wrought in nature. We are part of that nature. And part of being human is accepting the fact that "know we must"—just as generations before us pushed knowledge forward. To say that if we had not pursued *this* knowledge—splitting the atom—we would not be in this mess is an utter misunderstanding of the human condition. It is in using this knowledge to endanger or destroy the world that we have gone wrong. The question then becomes: where was that mistake made?

KNOWLEDGE VERSUS TECHNOLOGY

First of all, it seems that we need to differentiate knowledge from technology. They are not synonymous! Where we may consistently go wrong is not in striving to know all that we can possibly know, but rather in what we do with our knowledge. If there is a defect, that defect is in the motive of individuals to use knowledge for self-aggrandizement, whatever the long-range effects. Thus, as observed in Chapter 1, if greed and vested interests were not such powerful components of the arms race and its technological underpinnings, our knowledge of the atom would be so much less dangerous. There is nothing wrong with knowing, for instance, that we can convert uranium into plutonium. It is even conceivable that sometime in the future this knowledge may save us from extinction. But to construct breeder reactors in the face—let alone for the purpose—of creating chain reactions that are more than likely to pollute our environment and could very possibly blow up our world is an entirely different matter. True, without the knowledge we would not be in the predicament we are in. But it does not follow that we are in the predicament because of the knowledge. That is the fallacy of affirming the consequences and failing to look at our own responsibility in the use of knowledge.

Related to the double-edged issue of scientific/technological endeavor, and affecting it, is the prevailing attitude of human society toward nature. Rather than being regarded as a partner— sometimes cooperative, sometimes hostile and violent—in cosmic interdependence with all its creatures and specifically humanity, nature is seen as there to be mastered, conquered, and exploited primarily for human survival and comfort. Again, it is a question of balance and avoiding extremes. Certainly it is a good thing to use scientific and technological knowledge to promote human comfort and prevent the loss of life and property that lies in the wake of flooding, earthquakes, and so on. It is clear from the reports of disasters worldwide that poor countries who cannot afford the technology and equipment for warning and rescue clearly suffer much greater losses than are usual in technologically developed and wealthy nations (Wijkman and Timberlake 1984, Hoff 1989: 300–02). But besides being used beneficially, technology is also used—or abused—when the primary motive is not the safety and well-being of all, but serving the special interests of a few. Energy speculation, the multiplication of nuclear power plants, the failure to develop protections from hazardous waste— all of these are clear misuses of technology.

Let us return to our Frankenstein analogy: the good scientist starts out with the noblest intentions. After discovering the "astonishing secret" of the generation of life, Dr. Frankenstein elatedly declares that he will "pour a torrent of light into our dark world." But by some inexplicable mistake, his good intentions run amok. He creates a monster that he cannot control, and the creature turns against his creator, threatening continuous disaster unless Dr. Frankenstein will make the monster a companion of his own kind. Frankenstein agrees reluctantly and starts to create a female monster. But when the work is almost complete, he changes his mind—for fear that the two will people the world with monstrous offspring. The scientist destroys his second creation. The monster then carries out his murderous threats by killing Dr. Frankenstein's best friend and strangling the scientist's bride on their wedding night. At the end of the story, Frankenstein sets off in pursuit of his creation, determined to destroy the monster.

It is significant that Frankenstein was not fated to go on creating monsters. He could stop the process, just as we can stop the nuclear madness. And at the severest risk to himself—whatever the mistakes of the past—he did finally take charge of the future. Likewise, the careening advance of destruction—of technology run amok—can be stopped. Though we cannot unlearn what we have learned—though we will never again live in a pre-atomic age—we can take charge of our actions, restraining their negative potential while cultivating their positive ones. Compared to all the other planets we know anything about, Earth is still the Garden of Eden. If we lose Paradise this time around, it will be lost forever.

And why do we agonize so, when the solution to the dilemma is really very simple: get rid of all the arsenals of weapons, and stop building more sophisticated ones. What is the good of having weapons that once unleashed cannot be controlled—weapons that are utterly impartial in their course of destruction? Why does it seem almost beyond our power to put a halt to the ever-increasing danger of total annihilation? Perhaps it is because of the kind of people we have become. Perhaps it is because the modern mind-set is so unduly influenced by technology and an ideology in which materialism, competition, and narrow self-interest reign supreme. Einstein's appeal for a new mode of thinking demands a new mind-set. Our technology is geared to systematic problem-solving for its own sake, regardless of effect. In its place we desperately need a more global, ecological, qualitative approach to the problems that beset us—an approach akin to that of Nobel laureate Barbara McClintock who, studying kernels of corn, paid as much attention to the exceptional kernel as to the universals of the lot (Keller 1983a).

ATTITUDES TOWARD NATURE: CONQUEST OR COOPERATION?

Barbara McClintock's method of inquiry can serve as a model for the new mind-set needed in scientific pursuit—a model that emphasizes the nonexploitative attitude of working with, rather than mastery of, nature. Though McClintock's classic work in genetics and cytology began in the 1920s and 1930s, it was not recognized until many years later because she was a philosophical and methodological deviant. As her biographer Eveyln Fox Keller (1983a) notes, McClintock's approach militates against the omniscience, objectifiability, and ultimate control of nature on which classical science is based. Instead, her language about nature implies "affection, kinship, empathy"—an intimacy that questions the traditional boundaries between the knower and the known. In describing one of her breakthroughs in cytological (cell) analysis, McClintock describes the state of mind that enabled her to discover chromosomes she had not identified earlier:

I found that the more I worked with them, the bigger and bigger [the chromosomes] got, and when I was really working with them I wasn't outside . . . . I was part of the system . . . . I actually felt as if I was right down there and these were my friends . . . . As you look at these things, they become a part of you. And you forget yourself. (Keller 1983a, p. 105)

This "feeling for the organism" is a recognition of being part of that nature in which science is so profoundly interested. Such an attitude can replace the alienation that results when an "objective" observer is bent on investigating a completely separate entity. The very willingness to *consider* nuclear war as an answer to political differences implies the most profound disrespect of all of nature— mineral, plant, animal, and human.

The literature of violence research echoes this same theme. A necessary ingredient for violence is a perception of the other as object (Toch 1969). Accordingly, in hostage situations, time and communication are the greatest deterrents against destruction as they allow for a bond to develop between hostage and hostage-taker, transposing the hostage from object to subject. Human connectedness and commonalities then have some chance of re-placing the original motive for the hostage-taking—usually polit-ical (Hoff 1989:287). Similarly, in the arms race, indulging in argument over the "objective" number of comparable holdings only masks the human face of those who would be destroyed in a nuclear exchange, and serves only to escalate the race on the false premise that greater numbers will act as a deterrent.

We have come, then, to the brink of a second Paradise Lost. We got to where we are by way of two main threads meeting and intertwining at this particular moment in time. The first is the defect in our individual motives. Self-interest and traditional patterns of competitive behavior immobilize us in outmoded paradigms. At the same time, we have acquired a technology with the potential for global destruction. Neither of the two threads by itself is sufficient to cause our present condition. After all, greed has been around for many centuries. The two are necessary to bring about nuclear annihilation. Thus we need to untangle our technological know-how from our mind-set and value system—our present mode of thinking and acting. Given a new mind-set, we may yet become the masters of our knowledge, rather than its slave. We may begin to cooperate—rather than compete—with nature and our fellow human beings.

3

Prerequisites for Nuclear War

THE NECESSARY CONDITION

Just as nature is more complex than a set of universally observable laws, so is the process of arriving at the brink of nuclear destruction. What is terrifying, however, is that it may be all too simple to *start* a nuclear war. We shall attempt to sort out the events necessary and sufficient to ignite a nuclear war, in the hope that our understanding the process will help toward its reversal.

In the first place, nuclear annihilation can only occur if we or any other nation has the technology to make, deploy, and deliver nuclear bombs. Certainly, it is an undisputed fact that a number of countries do possess the necessary technology and that at least two nations have a nuclear arsenal large enough to incinerate the entire planet. Thus, the condition necessary for nuclear war does exist. But is this condition also sufficient to bring about nuclear disaster?

INITIATORS OF WAR VERSUS THE CRITICAL MASS

As far as we know, nuclear war does not spontaneously trigger itself. At least not to begin with. One or several human beings must take the initiative and set the event into motion: give the command; push the button; release the rockets. We the public really do not know whether one single individual is sufficient to start the whole thing going, or if the responsibility is shared: that is, the president may give the order; some other party relay it (hopefully not a computer); and a third party activate the system. It would seem that the more links necessary to set the war machine into motion, the better our chances that the chain may break and the process be blocked before it is too late. We do not know, since these most critical aspects concerning the survival of the human species and the Earth itself are shrouded in secrecy. This is another manifestation of the paternalistic leadership that would deny the people themselves a part in determining their own survival. Besides the political aspect of nuclear secrecy in which citizens may be persuaded that their government knows best, the sophistication of modern technology may in itself be so intimidating to the average person that it serves the purpose of keeping people uninformed.

However, the possession of a war arsenal—and even the readiness of initiators to start a war—may not be a sufficient condition for war to break out. At least, this is true as far as conventional wars are concerned. Without the consent of a vast majority willing to follow orders, wars can never be fought. One may wonder then how, throughout the ages, masses of people who were forcibly put into adverse, life-threatening situations did not simply refuse to fight. Only in the past 20 years has a sizeable resistance movement manifested itself. Probably the most likely explanation for the blind following of orders that often defied the most basic instincts of self-preservation was a general unawareness of existing alternatives. We are no longer unaware of alternatives, but one of the fundamental differences between a conventional war and a nuclear war is the possibility that the nuclear arsenal can be set off without our participation. At least, this is a widely held view, which goes a long way toward explaining the feelings of powerlessness and apathy that are attached to the subject of nuclear war.

Indeed, at least theoretically, just a handful of people could start and carry out nuclear destruction—utterly against the will of the rest of the world's population. Thus we are likely to feel that we have no role to play in preventing nuclear war. But in reality, an active resistance of a sufficient number of people—the all-important critical mass—may very well prevent its occurrence. A dramatic example of this kind was the U.S. withdrawal from Vietnam, which demonstrated how the determination and persistence of ordinary citizens—operating in opposition to war from the many different angles of their various circumstances—can prevail against even the most powerful central forces in government.

POWER OF THE CRITICAL MASS

It is important to understand the concept of "critical mass." Forcing the U.S. government to vacate Vietnam did not require that every single individual—and not even a majority of the population—object to government policy practices. Just as one atom added to a critical mass is all it takes to set off the chain reactions of nuclear fission, so too can one person—you, for instance—be the additional individual needed to reach the critical size (or critical mass) necessary to prevent nuclear war. Thus, any one of us may play the most decisive role in the critical affairs of society today.

Why then do we feel so powerless? One of our problems is a partly voluntary lack of imagination. It protects us from fully visualizing the "unthinkable" horrors of such a war. It also prevents us from insisting that government serve our mandates (which, after all, defines democracy)—rather than the other way around. Instead of searching for ways to prevent those who consider nuclear war a viable course of action from ever carrying it out, we engage in self-deceptive maneuvers as a protection against feeling inadequate, helpless, and anxious. Unfortunately, distorting or denying the gravity of our present condition does not change its reality. On the contrary, as already noted, it may even be instrumental in bringing about the disaster.

What complicates matters even more is that, on the one hand, we must face the fact that nuclear annihilation of the whole world as we know it is not only possible, but a likely occurrence if we continue on our present course. On the other hand, doomsaying about the likelihood of eventual annihilation may lead us even more directly to the fulfillment of that prophecy. However, there is a qualitative difference between believing we are fated for nuclear destruction, and sensitizing ourselves to the defense mechanisms that keep us passive and compliant. Admitting that we may very well be on the brink of self-destruction (via omnicide) is a necessary first step to effecting change in our present condition. As long as we deny its reality, we can have no control over it.

Somerville (1979) correctly identified the very idea of nuclear war as "nuclear omnicide"—the destruction of all living things, removing every possibility of transition to new living units.[1] Rather than preserving peace, "those who take no action against these weapons will, in effect, be casting their votes for omnicide" (Somerville 1979).

Our use of the term here focuses on the personality characteristics of a population that is passive in the face of global threat and seemingly content to leave the fate of the Earth in the hands of leaders who still rely on vast nuclear arsenals to maintain peace. In order to uncover the self-deceptive maneuvers we are all engaged in, we need first to describe these omnicidal personality characteristics so prevalent in our society, along with the most common defense mechanisms we have erected to protect ourselves from overwhelming nuclear-related anxieties.

THE OMNICIDAL PERSONALITY AND THE MECHANISMS OF DEFENSE

In our extensive research on attitudes toward nuclear threat (discussed more fully in succeeding chapters), we found some remarkable relationships between the very frequently occurring responses—even to the point of there being response syndromes— that are a reflection of a prevalent mind-set we have labeled "omnicidal." Thus, people who believe that nuclear war in their lifetime is either absolutely inevitable or—on the contrary—absolutely impossible, both maintain that they hardly ever think about it. They are also both likely to view nuclear war as causing only limited damage, and they are unwilling to invest any energy in efforts to prevent a nuclear disaster.

The first two seemingly opposite responses have dynamically the same effect: there is nothing one can do if nuclear war is inevitable, and nothing one needs to do if it cannot occur. Thus, it is not surprising that these people hardly ever think about it. Their disinclination to put any energy into its prevention was frequently explained by remarks such as: there is nothing I *can* do; I have no control over it; I'm just a little guy, I have no power; it's not my responsibility, our government will take care of it; I have full trust in our president (or God) to do the right thing. All of the above are manifestations of feelings of inadequacy, powerlessness, and lack of control over one's own destiny.

These are the very hallmarks of the omnicidal personality. We may define "omnicide" as the destruction of humanity by humanity. In further describing the omnicidal personality, the "sheep syndrome" may serve as a fitting analogy: whole herds of sheep have been known to drown in the flooding of rivers, for want of a shepherd to lead them to higher ground. At times they would have been saved by moving just a few yards, but instead they stood there and let it happen.

The consistent personality pattern of the omnicidal persuasion is marked by inaction, passivity, and apathy (seen in lack of participation in any preventive measures); dependence (expressed by trust in government, the president, God); lack of imagination and of knowledge (as in claiming that nuclear war cannot occur or that it would only cause limited damage); and fatalism (the overriding sense of no control over one's own destiny, and in this case the Earth's as well). The overuse of defense mechanisms is clearly evident in the omnicidal response pattern.

A brief review of the most typical defenses operating to support an omnicidal personality pattern may be helpful here. *Repression* and *denial of reality* are the most heavily relied on defenses when faced with the nuclear threat. In the response set described above, repression is expressed by a lack of preoccupation about nuclear issues: "I hardly ever think about the nuclear threat." Denial of reality is demonstrated in the belief that nuclear war cannot occur, or that damages of such a war would be limited in scope. Repression and denial can be expressed in many forms and usually combine with other defenses.

In *regression*, responsibility is shifted to an authority figure such as the president, with absolute trust that he will protect us from any possible catastrophe. As long as we have blind trust in "daddy," we face no danger. After the television film "The Day After" was aired, then–Secretary of State George Shultz addressed the nation paternalistically in a fireside chat of sorts to reassure viewers that things are not really so bad as the film portended. Basically, his message was that we of the government are in full charge, taking care of everything (even if—which went unsaid—it leads to our total destruction). Such displays simply reinforce a societal tendency toward a facsimile of childhood dependence in which parents protect their children from outside threats.

The defense of *projection* is shown by placing the blame for our nuclear dilemma on hostile forces, which—depending on one's persuasion—may be one's own government, communism, God, or the enemy.

Rationalization often takes the form of pseudo-scientific claims—such as the absolute necessity of our own extinction—that are positioned into the context of the supposed inevitable and lawful extinction of all species; or in a similar vein, the inevitability of nuclear war may be ascribed to "human nature," which is taken to be inherently aggressive and self-destructive and therefore doomed to self-annihilation. The fact that extinct species have usually succumbed to external, cataclysmic events over which they had no control is not taken into account here.

An ever-increasing phenomenon we are confronted with all the time lately is the devaluation of life, which can be explained in terms of *reaction formation*. Life is experienced as undesirable, and the threat of total annihilation is seen as an indifferent or even desirable prospect. Thus, one is protected against the horror of nuclear war; there is nothing to lose. The devaluation of life may be accompanied by a flight into supernatural beliefs, with some form of heaven or "life-after-life" representing the most ideal goal to strive for. In extreme cases, individuals will even advocate the destruction of our planet to bring about apocalyptic promises. Here the omnicidal tendencies—allowing total annihilation through passivity—resemble defenses sometimes observed in the case of individual self-destruction: my suicide will hasten my eternal reward; I have suffered enough; life in the hereafter must be better than what I endure here. (In Chapter 6 we make a more detailed distinction between omnicide and suicide).

Another commonly encountered reality-denying defense is *escape* or *fantasy*, often reflected in a hedonistic, planless life-style. Many of our present-day ills may be better understood as reactions to the nuclear threat. Thus, devaluation of life as a sign of hopelessness may help explain the steady increase in suicides, as well as the decrease in the age of suicide victims; the escape of many to the oblivion of alcohol and other drugs; and the general abandonment of the old and the disadvantaged in society. Two decades ago, preadolescent suicides and drug abuse were almost unheard of. Now they are an everyday occurrence. Psychologically, these young people feel despair; socially, they experience a growing alienation from significant others and a sense of purpose. But devaluation of life is not only inner but also outer directed. When one's own life loses its value, so does one's neighbor's life. Violence is rampant in many neighborhoods and in many families, and many cite fear of violence as a primary concern (Hoff 1989: 244–49). In many acts of violence, victims are seen by their assailants as mere objects to be destroyed for whatever temporary gain or tension relief may be secured.

Alienation, then, is a response to overwhelming nuclear anxiety: if I isolate myself from all human attachments, then I will have no losses to fear. Avoidance of commitment, disintegration of the family as a stable structure, lack of empathy, and the tendency toward violence can all be explained in terms of alienation. Its specific impact on youth is the topic of Chapter 4.

II

The Effect of Nuclear Threat on Our Lives

4

The Impact of the Nuclear
Threat on Youth

ADOLESCENT IDENTITY CRISIS

We are observing the most disturbing phenomena nationally among our adolescent population in terms of ever-increasing drop-out rates, lack of interest—let alone enthusiasm—in anything but immediate need gratification, avoidance of commitment and responsibility, and finally a devaluation of life itself as seen in escalating acts of violence against others as well as against themselves. "Alienation" has become a catchall word for these dismal manifestations, and the blame seems to have shifted from the educational system to the parents, and back again to the educational system. There is no doubt that alienation is a prevailing feeling—not only among the young, but among all age groups. And all our social institutions—including the family and educational systems—are implicated in their deleterious effect on adolescents. But there has been a general failure to acknowledge the most disturbing factor influencing the alienation of young and old alike: living with the threat of total annihilation.

Our assumption here is that the nuclear threat is all pervasive, affecting every aspect of our lives—especially during tumultuous life-cycle changes when people are more vulnerable than usual. Thus, the possibility of no tomorrow has far-reaching effects on adolescents, who are in a most significant transitional stage between who they have been and who they are becoming. Indeed, their very existence depends on the projection of who they will become in the future. Adolescence implies "liminality": it is an in-between state in which the person is neither child nor adult. We have been well aware of the vicissitudes of the adolescent identity crisis for some time now, even before the continuation of life was so overwhelmingly threatened. Paul Goodman (1960) captured this phenomenon in his description of adolescents "growing up absurd," struggling with their relative uselessness between the child and adult statuses. Actually, adolescence itself is a recently defined stage of development that marks a departure from the traditional social structure in which roles were more rigidly defined and young people assumed adult responsibilities concomitant with sexual maturity.

Without a secure future, one cannot acquire—let alone maintain—one's self-identity. Having no future also means having no connectedness, being detached from all the necessary bonds with family and friends, experiencing no possibility of extending beyond oneself, one's family, and whatever it is that one cherishes to the larger community. Instead, the future looms as nothingness. Phyllis LaFarge highlights young people's thwarted sense of the future by citing a poem from a theater piece used in peace-awareness sessions:

> What's the use of going to college?
> What's the use of making money?
> What's the use of preparing for a future?
> When I have none?
> What's the use of loving if the people I love are going to die?
> Before I can ever express my love for them?
> What's the use of living?
> I feel as though I'm dead right now.
> My grave was dug
> Before I was even born. (LaFarge 1987: 14)

The life-style of the young—so much decried—is but a logical consequence of the feeling of futurelessness. With very possibly no tomorrow, life turns planless. All energy must be invested in today—thus the emphasis on living for the moment (quite different from the existential living *in* the moment). Young people daydream of future accomplishments that will bring them the attention—if not admiration—they crave from their parents, teachers, and peers, along with the envy of their foes. With their hopes for eventually realizing these dreams shaken, there remains the craving for highs, for thrills, for excitement that must be satisfied right now—or it never will be. As one young man put it,

Well, I think the general effect on me is my lack of believing that there is some kind of future. And I live my life that way . . . . I've been through three wives—and I have a sailboat and I used to race cars. I know how to have fun . . . . Susan and I are going to get married . . . and we hope to have a couple of kids. A lot of younger people say to me, "What are you going to do that for; you're going to raise them up in this world?" And I say, "Well, I'll make my world the way I want it, and if it's not okay, I'll go somewhere where it can be okay. I'll get on a sailboat." (LaFarge 1987: 22)

Unfortunately, the young rarely have a legitimate outlet for their cravings, other than in preparation and hopes for the future. But excitement and immediate highs can be gained by engaging in forbidden activities such as stealing cars, vandalism, and the use of alcohol or other drugs. Notoriety can be gained by committing crimes or attempting suicide. Eric Chivian, a psychiatrist at the Massachusetts Institute of Technology, raises the question, "What is it like to grow up without believing that you will?" And Chivian concludes that it may be too much to expect kids who feel that way to work hard in school, develop deep relationships, or do anything that assumes there is a future (Yudkin 1984). And if these everyday challenges are overwhelming for many young people, staying alive without a vision for the future is the most basic challenge of all.

(Later we analyze in more detail the increase in youth suicides in relation to nuclear threat.)

There has been some controversy regarding children's awareness of the nuclear threat and of its impact on their lives. Thus, Robert Coles (1985) suggests that, left to themselves, children have scant concern for the possibility of nuclear war. He says that the children who have taken this issue to heart are from well-off families whose parents are involved in the nuclear freeze movement. Coles reached his conclusions after engaging in conversation with a number of children. For instance, Coles asked a 12-year-old boy whether the subject of nuclear bombs comes to his mind at any time. Does he hear his friends talk about it? Does he have any thought at all about the subject? And the 12 year old answered, "Well, sir, I don't give the nuclear bomb much thought, no sir."

Though we too found this response to be rather typical for children at that age, it is also susceptible to misinterpretation without further analysis. Our own research, as well as the findings of other investigators, has clearly shown that the impact of the nuclear threat on children as young as five years old can be overwhelming and may have devastating consequences on their developing life-style.[1] The more recent work of LaFarge (1987) documents extensively the consciousness and responses of children to the nuclear threat, and presents a powerful counterargument to Coles's assertion of nuclear anxieties being based on class differences. Jerald Backman's study (with Lloyd Johnston) of social trends among thousands of high school seniors revealed a fourfold increase between 1975 and 1984 in those who often worried about the chance of nuclear war (cited in LaFarge 1987: 27). Scott Haas's work among teens from different class groups not only refutes the Coles claim that nuclear anxiety is focused among middle- and upper-class youth, but also reveals that 82 percent of working- and lower-class teenagers expect to see a nuclear war during their lifetime—in contrast to only 29 percent in the other groups (cited in LaFarge 1987: 45). Similarly, Sibylle Escalona (1965) and Haas found that the poorest children were the *most* pessimistic about the future. Rather than daily survival issues of the poor consuming their "leeway for moral reflection," poverty and prejudice are added to nuclear war as "morally compelling issues" among racial minorities and low-income groups (LaFarge 1987: 44–45).

As LaFarge observes, many of these studies are criticized for faulty methodology such as a bias in sampling, or the presentation of leading questions. We agree with John Mack and W. R. Beardslee (1982) and others who acknowledge that there are problems in *every* kind of study, and that no research is value free. Also, while leading questions may bias research results, we can also err by failing to take seriously the real concerns of children. In fact, a key complaint among many young people is that adults do not listen to them and often doubt their veracity. The point of value-laden research like this is not to prove or claim a causal relationship between alienated youth and the fear of nuclear war. Rather, it is to explicate the complexity of young people's concerns within the *context* of nuclear realities and global threat and their influence on individual consciousness and behavior.

DEVELOPMENTAL CHANGES IN ATTITUDES

Our own investigations, which involved administering a questionnaire (Figure 4.1) among 410 elementary school children and 69 high school students, shed further light on the complexity of their reactions. It also allowed us to trace the gradual development of omnicidal characteristics: passivity, apathy, dependence on others to solve problems, fatalism, and an overly defensive posture. In presenting some of our research results here, our aim is to convey major tendencies and changes in the developing awareness of nuclear realities, rather than reiterate the statistical details found in the original reports (Goodman 1987).

We found that the most dramatic change in reactions to the nuclear threat occurs during the first four years of elementary school, between the ages of six and ten. Surprisingly, almost all of the first-grade children we interviewed in two inner cities claimed

Figure 4.1
Children's Questionnaire

```
AGE: _____        SEX: _____

GRADE: _____      SCHOOL: _____
```

1. Have you heard of "Nuclear War"?
    (1) Yes ____   (2) No ____   (3) Not sure ____

2. Who has talked to you about a Nuclear War and who did
    you hear talk about it?
    (1) a parent (mother or father) ____   (4) teacher ____
    (2) family member ____   (5) television ____
    (3) friends ____   (6) other ____

3. Is there going to be a Nuclear War in your lifetime?
    (1) I think so ____ (2) Don't think so ____ (3) I can't say ____

4. What would a Nuclear War do to you?
    (1) Not too much ____   (3) kill my family ____
    (2) kill me ____   (4) other ____

5. Can you do something to prevent a Nuclear War?
    (1) Yes ____   (2) No ____

6. Who can do something to prevent a Nuclear War?
    (1) parents (mother, father) ____   (4) Russia ____
    (2) the president of U.S.A. ____   (5) other ____
    (3) a lot of people ____

7. How old do you think you will get?
    (1) die before you are 100 ____ (2) die before you are 60 ____
    (3) die before you are 30 ____   (4) other age ____

8. Did you ever dream of being in Nuclear War?
    (1) Yes ____   (2) No ____

9. What would life be like after a Nuclear War?
    (1) good ____   (4) no life ____
    (2) terrible ____   (5) other ____
    (3) fun-adventurous ____

10. Would you want to be alive after a Nuclear War?
    (1) Yes ____   (2) No ____

that they did not know the meaning of "nuclear war" and that they had never heard anyone talk about it. But when asked if it makes them think of candy, school, bombs, balloons, or soldiers, all of them associated it with bombs. Further ignoring their professed ignorance on the topic, we inquired what a nuclear war would do to them. They all expressed the belief that it would kill people—in most cases not themselves, but their parents and/or everybody else. Feelings of omnipotence were expressed in an almost unanimous belief in their own power to do something to prevent a nuclear war.

Only 3 of the 24 first- and second-graders who were asked that question had as much confidence in their parents' power. On the other hand, the president, a lot of people, and even the Soviet Union were chosen a number of times as possible preventers of a nuclear war. One child said that only God can prevent it. At this stage, children's trust in the future is still intact. None of our interviewees thought that there will be a nuclear war in their lifetime. Perhaps the most startling revelation came in response to a question on dreams about nuclear war they may have had. Half of these first-graders spoke of nightmarelike dreams—all of them death related, with "being left alone" as the most frequently occurring theme. The children were unanimous in their desire to survive a nuclear war, though they thought that life would be terrible or that there would be no life at all.

The contradictions encountered at this level of development are most interesting: almost all of the children we interviewed voiced ignorance when first confronted with the topic. Yet their appropriate associations demonstrate awareness of the nuclear threat. It is still a vague concept, which seems to evoke anxiety in dreams. At the second-grade level, nuclear war has become a familiar subject; television is the leading source of information, followed by teacher. Parents are the least frequently mentioned as a source of information. The most plausible explanation for parents sharing so little information is the "pact of silence" cited by LaFarge (1987: 97–122). While parents' manifest motive in remaining silent is the protection of their children, their silence also supplies children with a model of behavior about nuclear issues and lays the foundation for omnicidal personality characteristics and denial as a way of coping with nuclear-related anxieties.

Among our second-graders, remembering nightmarelike dreams about nuclear war reached an all-time high, with only two children not remembering having had such dreams. In all other respects, their responses do not differ from those of the younger children, with whom they still share feelings of omnipotence and optimism: there will be no nuclear war in their lifetime. Response homogeneity breaks down at the third-grade level. Thus, responses from eight year olds cannot be predicted on the basis of age alone.

Their views on nuclear war have become more realistic: only 7 of the 27 third-graders we interviewed share the younger children's optimistic belief in no nuclear war in their lifetime. The rest split evenly between thinking there will be nuclear war and responding "I can't say." Furthermore, they do not share the unanimously expressed desire of the first- and second-graders to survive a nuclear war; only 37 percent expressed such a preference. We also get the first inkling of the use of repression as a defense against nuclear-related anxiety: more than one-third of the third-graders we interviewed no longer remember having had dreams about being in a nuclear war. This is in stark contrast to the experiences of the seven year olds, who—almost without exception—gave minute reports on their terror-filled dreams.

The most significant and enduring changes occur at the fourth-grade level, when children's feelings of power and confidence are apparently fast eroding. The majority of fourth-graders participating in this study no longer believe that they can do anything to help prevent a nuclear war. This feeling of powerlessness increases through high school, where 76 percent of the students voice their inability to play any role in the prevention of a nuclear war. At the same time, among fourth-graders the belief that nuclear war will occur in their lifetime steadily increases; the desire to survive a nuclear war decreases, with a more realistic awareness of its consequences. While all the first- and second-graders voiced their preference to be alive after a nuclear war, only 30 percent of fourth-graders would opt to survive such a war.

Repression is becoming more clearly manifest: 75 percent of our fourth-graders no longer remember any nuclear war dreams. Interestingly, there is an orderly progression of not remembering nuclear war dreams that starts in the third grade; at the college level, only 15 percent of students recall ever having dreamt about being in a nuclear war. These responses parallel the students' increasing sense of powerlessness and inability to prevent a nuclear war. And they evoke the image of what LaFarge (1987:

74–75) calls the "survival artist," who "will not feel and therefore not do" and who thus withdraws from the democratic process—in short, an omnicidal personality. LaFarge also associates this withdrawal process with technology and the mysteries of such things as strategic defense systems, which evoke helplessness because they seem unaccountable and beyond individual influence (pp. 82–89).

We have also tapped repressive defenses by asking questions that deal with the frequency of thinking about the possibility of nuclear annihilation. We did not use this question in interviews with children under ten years of age. However, interviews with older children confirmed an increasing use of repression, peaking at adolescence. On the two extremes of the dimension—thinking almost daily about nuclear annihilation or never (hardly ever) thinking about it—more than half of the 10–14 year olds reported almost daily preoccupation with the nuclear war issue; in contrast, only 2 percent of 14–16 year olds claimed daily preoccupation. (In the adult population, about 10 percent make the same claim.)

At the other end of the dimension, only 10 percent of the 10–14 year olds say that they never, or hardly ever, think about nuclear war—in contrast to 75 percent of the 14–16 year olds. Cross-culturally, in a 1984 Swedish study among 13–15 year olds, 42 percent indicated that their greatest concern was nuclear war (Holmborg and Bergstrom 1984). In an informal survey by a team of U.S. psychiatrists in 1983, 60 Soviet young people between the ages of 10 and 15 were interviewed on videotape, and 293 responded to a written questionnaire. This segment of Soviet youth were found to be less optimistic than U.S. youth about survival in a nuclear war, but more optimistic about the prevention of war (Chivian and Goodman 1984). (Less than half of the adult populations we interviewed deny any preoccupation with nuclear war, while—as noted above—about 10 percent claim daily preoccupation with the issue.)

A quantitative as well as a more qualitative analysis of our interviews clearly indicates the gradual development of omnicidal personality characteristics among U.S. youth concomitant with a developing defensive structure. In a dozen personal interviews with kindergartners and first-graders, we found each and every one of them eager to express their thoughts and fears on any aspect of the subject we broached. Though the term "nuclear war" was not in their vocabulary, the devastating images of nuclear destruction and death played a very dominant part in their mental life. As already noted, a dominant fear among children at this age is the loss or destruction of their parents—which is true even in the absence of nuclear threat. For children, then, living in the nuclear age seems to add another dimension to common childhood fears.

Interestingly, in every case where a child had experienced a personal loss—the death of a parent, a sibling, or a pet—she or he would divert our focus of discussion and talk about that loss. With the exception of the death of a pet, no one in their family had discussed the traumatic experience with the child, suggesting that death is still very much a taboo topic in U.S. society. Asked if they would want to talk about it, the children always said they would but added something like "it would make Mommy too sad," implying the pact of silence that LaFarge speaks of and a certain role reversal in which children feel responsible to protect their parents. Experiences like these at this developmental stage may well lay the foundation for repression, denial of reality, and the need of young people to withdraw from both a family and a society they perceive as too threatening or indifferent to their needs.

Our findings indicate clearly that young children lack omnicidal characteristics: the feeling of power to help prevent a nuclear disaster erodes only slowly; and with it, preoccupation with the nuclear threat diminishes. Young children have a rich fantasy life, with no lack of imagination—as attested to in their vivid dreams. How does it get lost? Perhaps we learn to avoid, suppress, and eventually repress the horror-filled images of nuclear reality. With our loss of childhood feelings of empowerment, lack of imagination becomes a protection.

Unfortunately, lack of imagination protects us only from our fantasies, however. To protect ourselves from reality, we must first face it. The response of the 12-year-old boy who told Robert Coles

(1985) that he doesn't give the bomb much thought comes as no surprise to us, then. We observed that the manifestation of certain omnicidal characteristics—including repression—increase rapidly after the age of ten. In the course of our extended research in which more than 1,400 people of diverse nationalities and widely differing socio-economic backgrounds were surveyed, the one definite picture that emerged is that of an enormous complexity and instability with regard to attitudes toward the nuclear threat. Aside from the developmental changes discussed above, personal as well as national circumstances in interaction with deep-seated personality characteristics—including gender—influence and change our reactions toward life in the nuclear age. We do, however, find remarkable agreement among the major research efforts in this field, when age, gender, and ethical-political values are kept constant (see especially LaFarge 1987). As already suggested, the pitfalls of oversimplification lead to conclusions such as Coles (1985) reported when he said that children left to themselves have scant concern with the possibility of nuclear war, and that the children who have taken this issue to heart are from "well-off" families involved in the nuclear freeze movement.

The phrase "children left to themselves" is itself ambiguous. Could it mean that such children have not been influenced by their parents regarding nuclear issues? But our own research, as well as that of others (Schwebel 1965, Mack and Beardslee 1982, LaFarge 1987), shows even more fear and apprehension among children whose parents do not share their own worries with the kids. Indeed, the least fearful children are those whose parents are actively engaged in opposing nuclear war. As we discuss more fully in Part III, not only are such children less fearful; they also feel empowered through their parents' activism, which blends with the support and encouragement a developing person needs (see Yudkin 1984, LaFarge 1987). When Coles contrasts children "left to themselves" with those of "well-off" families, he implies a class difference. If he is referring in the first instance to children from broken homes, hungry children, abused children, and/or children growing up in slums where survival may be a daily preoccupation, then indeed we will not find that their primary concern is with nuclear issues. There is a great deal of evidence that children, as well as adults, whose immediate personal safety or survival is at stake see this as the most compelling issue on their mind. But just because nuclear war is not their *first* concern, we should not conclude that it is of *no* concern. As LaFarge points out, "For the poor, the presence of the threat of nuclear war is one more dark element in a picture of the world already made dark by their position in society" (1987: 45).

It would therefore be an oversimplification to state that the threat of nuclear annihilation has a greater effect on those who are well-off than on those who are not. Results of a pilot study we conducted in 1982 with different socio-economic groups concur with the work of LaFarge regarding class and nuclear anxieties. In one sample, we asked 35 college students—20 of them from Harvard—whether the threat of nuclear annihilation influences the way they lead their life, and their plans for the future. It was a semi-open question, with the following choices:

1. Yes. It has influenced my life. I live from day to day. I don't plan for the future.
2. Yes. I turned against the establishment; I do my own thing while it lasts.
3. I try to live as if humankind will find a solution.
4. It has no influence on my life.
5. Other (explain).

Of the 20 Harvard students, 14 responded that they try to live as if a solution will be found; four said that it has no influence on their lives; one said that she has turned against the establishment; and one stated that it has influenced her not in terms of turning against the establishment, but in terms of investing all her energy to help save the Earth. Of the 15 students at an urban state college who were also surveyed, only six said that they live as if a solution will be found; five felt that it has no influence on their lives; and four stated that they have turned against the establishment and are doing their own thing while it lasts.

We used the same question with 36 high school and college dropouts and with 17 young people at a methadone clinic, with very different results. The vast majority claimed that the threat of nuclear war has greatly influenced their lives, and blamed it for all the negative turns their lives have taken. Though there are some variations in their stories, there is also one common theme: they had dropped out of school, from careers, and/or from intimate relationships because any effort or sacrifice demanded to further such commitments seems wasted in light of their sense of futurelessness.

Though the young people in the latter group were primarily from a low socio-economic class and to a great extent from culturally deprived homes, we also encountered a great many young "social dropouts" who came from highly advantaged, professional, idealistic homes. And their reasons for turning their backs on possible accomplishments, careers, and commitments were often similar to those of their socially deprived contemporaries. This finding unveils some of the mystery and public consternation regarding suicides among young persons who appear to have "everything going for them." Clearly, a fair number of them decide that death has more to offer than what they envision as awaiting them in adulthood (Hoff 1990b).

But again, not all young people who turn their back on the establishment and our societal values are self-indulgent hedonists who have given up on life and the future. They may just be the forerunners of a generation that must acquire a new mind-set if we are to survive (to invoke Einstein again). We refer here to the movement that was in full swing in the 1960s when young idealists all over the country renounced competition, aggression, and exploitation of others as well as of the environment, and chose a very different life-style—often resorting to all-sharing communal living arrangements.

It is far beyond the scope of this book to delve into all the positive as well as negative motivations that drove so many into such an altered life-style. But we see the underlying dynamics of the movement closely related to life in the nuclear age, a despair with the elder exploitive generation that may very well have robbed them of their future. While much is said about the materialistic attitude of young people today, this trend needs to be seen in the context of a similar attitude among adults. Why should young people be faulted for their hedonism or their failure to choose service professions over making money, when the primary models they observe in adults stress the latter? Yet, a new consciousness appears to be on the horizon, embodied in the new age movement. This countertrend that stirred to life in the 1980s emphasizes the limits of a consumer mentality in satisfying people's needs for peace and inner harmony, and it is a movement that dovetails with peace and environmental activities. In Part III we suggest ways that disillusioned young people might be engaged in such activities and in a life-style that portends more hope for the future.

In spite of the many prevalent negative characteristics of Western cultures—such as self-interest, greed, aggressiveness, and materialism—there are many other cultural aspects of Western societies that its members can be proud of. Our "most cherished" list would include individualism, independence, self-reliance, and creativity (by which we mean all that has been accomplished beyond our animal level of existence). However, the downside of individualism—for instance—is that family and community values may be sacrificed to an extent unimaginable in societies where communal concerns outweigh those of individuals.

In the nuclear era we are severely divided by what has been commonly called the "generation gap"—which we believe has much less to do with age differences than with having been born either into the relatively secure pre-nuclear era or into the post-nuclear era, with the fate of the Earth in balance at every moment. If one has never known anything else but an uncertain future—or rather the possibility of no future at all—the world is a very different place than if the future and all its generations to come have been a stable reference point that could be taken for granted.

The cultural mandate that we make every effort to preserve and expand our legacy and to pass it on to posterity has been one of the main goals of every civilized society. Part of the elation we experience when reading a literary masterpiece, watching one of the great stage dramas, contemplating the Acropolis or the Taj Mahal, or listening to Beethoven's symphonies comes from their timelessness and their universality. What affects us so deeply goes far beyond the momentary aesthetic pleasure. What affects us is the connection we experience with all humankind, with all those who came before us and those who will follow us. The idea that everything we cherish most in this life—the stuff that gives true meaning to our life—will disappear forever makes all our creative accomplishments senseless.

Our present experiences are embedded in past experiences and expectations of experiences yet to come. This is somewhat analogous to Edmund Husserl's (1913) "stream of experience," which describes existence as a chain linking consciousness to "retention" (past experiences) and "protention" (expectation of future experience)—with no impression possible without both retention and protention. Thus, the stream of experiences cannot start or end. Expanding on Husserl's idea we suggest that, without being anchored to the future through our legacy to posterity, the very essence of humanness is lost. Life becomes devoid of all meaning. The difference between the pre- and the post-nuclear generations lies in the way they relate to the world. The former knew a priori of existence as a link in a chain that extended from past into future. We have not been very successful in revising this image of the world. As a matter of fact, the end of our world is unthinkable. And our well-established defense mechanisms have been fairly successful in protecting us from overthrowing that image of a stable world in which we are the link between past and future. Thus, most of us who grew up in the pre-nuclear era cannot incorporate the possibility of planetary death into our experience of life.

It is also hard for us to imagine growing up in a world that in many respects is totally different from the one we grew up in. Not only has our most stable dimension of time been shifted by the possible loss of a future, but the second intuitional category that had anchored and described our world—space—has also undergone changes so drastic that, though we can grasp these changes intellectually—or at least some of our scientists can—it now bears little resemblance to our familiar perception of moving in a circumscribed world with above, below, and beyond as fairly stable reference points. The young have been born into a different space and time, and seem to be much more at home looking at our Earth as if they stood outside it—from the vantage point of seeing it as a planet among other planets. They seem to breach millions of light years with no more effort than it takes us to conceptualize the preceding or the next century. Star-swallowing black holes are no more magic to them than a whirlpool is to us.

By this, we do not mean to say that young people have a better grasp of astrophysics. On the contrary, very few have the intellectual understanding of the great scholars who made the dimensional breakthroughs in the first place. But they do have a perspective on time and space that is far more in line (or syntonic) with present-day technology than do those of us who were born in the pre-nuclear era.

Thus far, we who would be the keepers (and transmitters) of the culture have not seriously attempted to understand—and even less to accept—the utter shift in our society's hierarchy of values. Almost every issue of the education journals contains articles on the increasing lack of interest in all things literary, and on the deteriorating performance of students in communication skills. The need to master a language—even one's own—seems to have disappeared.

We know from firsthand experience that there are students in our accredited colleges of the Western culture who do not know who Shakespeare is, and only a few can name—let alone have read—more than three of his plays. A small minority know Shaw, and hardly anyone has ever heard of Goethe. Half the time Richard

Wagner is mistaken for Robert Wagner the movie actor. We feel that many precious aspects of our cultural inheritance are slipping from our grasp, and we seem incapable of communicating the importance of such a momentous loss to our students. At first we joked and then despaired over the clamor for "relevance"—which stands for all that is necessary and expedient in obtaining immediate goals, and resists the learning of anything so general and "irrelevant" as mathematics, reading, writing, and a critical examination of what history and philosophy can teach about the present day. And finally we educators have come to the conclusion that today's youth are sliding toward illiteracy—that we are witnessing the shrinking of the mind in Western society. Much of the blame has been directed against television for having replaced books and daydreams, and against the computer for having replaced thinking.

How did we fail to transmit our romantic involvement and appreciation of literature and the arts to the young? Perhaps there are limits to all human potentials, and an expansion in one direction brings about constriction in another. Perhaps Hamlet's problems or Julia's love—even when expressed in most melodious language—seem of little consequence to a generation of young men and women who on the one hand believe that they may have no say whatsoever on global questions of being or not being, and who on the other hand have a far more expanded time/space perspective to be overwhelmed by the bonding of two young lovers. We need to realize that we cannot expect the young to see the world from our pre-nuclear perspective. They have never been where we have been. But we are where they are—and we are responsible for it. If we do not come to terms with their view of the world, alienation and resentment between our generations will grow; and we will miss the opportunity to bring about the change in our mind-set and in theirs on which the very survival of our planet depends. The concern of most researchers involved with nuclear issues is a pragmatic one. It is not enough to formulate questions, look at statistics, and test theories. We are faced with a deadline. We must solve the nuclear dilemma before it is too late. If we can find no solution to this problem, there will be no other problems clamoring for our attention. Unfortunately, there are no shortcuts. Before we can effect a change in the ways we think, feel, and act—that is, a change in attitude—we need to understand our presently held attitudes.

The ABC-TV movie "The Day After" afforded a unique opportunity for researchers in this field not only to assess present-day attitudes, but also to observe the attitudinal effects of the media.

5

Attitudes toward Nuclear War

THE MEDIA EFFECT

In November 1983, as soon as ABC announced the impending television movie "The Day After," a vehement controversy broke out about the merits and desirability of airing such a show. The conflicting views became rapidly politicized. One side hailed the lifting of the taboo on nuclear awareness, while the other side feared that anti–nuclear war propaganda—which the film was sure to arouse—would change public sentiment from supporting deterrence to endorsing disarmament.

At this time the nuclear freeze movement was well under way. A number of countries and towns had collected a sufficient number of votes to declare their areas nuclear free zones, and anti-nuclear demonstrators in Europe as well as in a few U.S. cities were causing the establishment to worry about its being the sole remaining guardian of the fate of the Earth. Well-known conservatives and pro-defense organizations threatened to boycott U.S. businesses that ran ads during the show, and tried to persuade all major advertisers not to buy commercial time on that channel. William Buckley, the noted conservative journalist, wrote an article ridiculing the whole enterprise; while Jerry Falwell, head of the Moral Majority, called the program "a threat to our national security." One of the authors found a tape in her office mailbox, put there by a "born again" student whose minister had recorded a hellfire-and-brimstone sermon warning his flock of "Satan, who was coming through the tube, sent by the Russian bear, to assail America through the demons of fear . . . fear of nuclear war just to put us in bondage." But the minister assured his faithful that they need not fear the day after (the nuclear holocaust); they only need fear "the day after Christ comes back."[1]

ABC received mounting pressure about the film. On the one hand, conservatives urged them not to air it. On the other hand, the activities of anti-nuclear groups all over the country—aimed at encouraging people to watch "The Day After"—added enormous publicity to the film.

Rather than becoming intimidated, ABC launched a monumental campaign in which it sent out innumerable press releases, distributed hundreds of thousands of colorful viewers' guides, and held advanced viewings for the press, educators, and social scientists. The result of all this publicity campaigning was an audience of 100 million people—the largest audience, in fact, ever to watch a TV movie.

A further consequence of all this focus on a nuclear war film was that one could finally broach a topic that had heretofore been taboo with a large segment of the population. Certainly no school principal would have ever before given permission to question young people on their thoughts and feelings about the nuclear threat. But weeks before the film was aired, anti-war groups initiated discussions with teachers and parents to alert them to the severe anxiety-arousing effect that "The Day After" was expected to have on young children, recommending that very young children not be permitted to watch the show and advising them on how to handle children's fears about nuclear war. The organization Ground Zero alone circulated more than 300,000 viewers' guides in hundreds of cities all over the United States to warn people of the emotional impact that the film might have. The message was, "Watch the film . . . . But don't watch it alone." In any case, because of all the propaganda for and against viewing "The Day After" the topic could no longer be avoided by anyone. This fact alone helped to remove obstacles that had stood in the way of gaining a better understanding of people's attitudes toward nuclear war.

We had been baffled for a long time at the relative calm with which the majority of people all over the world seemed to have accepted that the worst imaginable event ever to befall humankind might possibly happen during their lifetime: a nuclear holocaust. Until recently, almost no attempt had been made by private citizens to halt the ever-increasing threat of nuclear war. Anti-nuclear activists held demonstrations, conferences, and teach-ins at which they were talking to each other—the already converted—but seemingly without reaching the rest of the population. As a matter of fact, the meetings had a strong in-group flavor; the personal pronouns "us" and "them" showed up in almost everything said. "Them" stood primarily for the establishment, but also for all the people who failed to show any overt concern about the nuclear threat. However, a grass-roots movement that enlists the support of all kinds of people is certainly required to change our ways of thinking and relating toward each other, if the world is to be saved from destruction.[2]

But to achieve the change in attitude necessary to a universal resistance against all nuclear threat, we must first of all understand the reasons why a vast majority do not make any effort to halt the approaching catastrophe that would maim or destroy whatever each and every one of us cherishes most in life—be it personal well-being, fellow creatures, nature, music, poetry, our planet.

How can we explain this apparent passivity in the face of planetary destruction? Is it general apathy or a feeling of powerlessness? Hopelessness or a lack of imagination? Perhaps people do not really believe that nuclear destruction is a possibility. Perhaps they cannot grasp the consequences of such a war. Perhaps they do not care or they just do not think about it, allowing the press of daily survival to occupy primary attention.

STUDY OF NUCLEAR ATTITUDES

To find answers to these and other questions, we designed a research instrument that includes a Likert-type Nuclear Attitude

Scale and a Nuclear War Questionnaire, and conducted a pilot study with the participation of 75 individuals. This early research has grown into an ongoing study of the development and change in attitudes toward nuclear war, involving more than 1,500 respondents in the United States and Western Europe. The TV show "The Day After" presented us with the opportunity to address these questions and to study the influence of the media and other consciousness-raising events on people's attitudes (Goodman 1984).

The findings presented here are based on the assessment of attitudes derived from the attitude scale, the questionnaire, and interviews of 259 respondents before they viewed the TV show and of 222 respondents after viewing the TV show. Of these, 124 respondents took part in both the before and after conditions, 135 took part in only the before condition, and 98 took part in only the after condition. The respondents included two groups of women and two groups of men ages 15–30 and 31–65 in each of the before and after conditions.

Findings from the Attitude Scale

The seven-point Nuclear Attitude Scale (see Figure 5.1)—consisting of ten items—assesses an individual's overall attitude toward nuclear war. It is based on the strength and direction of agreeing or disagreeing with each of the items. The possible range of scores is from +30 to -30. Anti-nuclear attitudes are revealed by plus scores, while pro-nuclear attitudes are revealed by minus scores.

Analysis of the data revealed a statistically significant increase in anti-nuclear scores after viewing "The Day After," in all but the group of older males in the correlation sample (see Table A.1 and A.2 in the Appendix). The following gender difference emerged:

1. Women in all four groups score higher on anti-nuclear attitudes than men do.

Figure 5.1
Nuclear Attitude Scale

Strongly Agree	Agree	Mildly Agree		Mildly Disagree	Disagree	Strongly Disagree
3	2	1	0	1	2	3

1. Nuclear annihilation is an abstract concept; it has no base in reality for me.

2. As long as we have nuclear missiles in Europe, the danger to our own country is lessened.

3. If the only choice is between unilateral nuclear disarmament or nuclear war, disarmament is the better choice.

4. Any consequence is better than the destruction of our planet.

5. The survival of future generations is more important than the continuation of our form of government.

6. If there is a nuclear confrontation, I would feel relieved to know that some parts of the world would be spared, even if it is not ours.

7. All we need is first-strike capacity to feel safe in a dangerous world.

8. We must be willing to run the risk of nuclear war to prevent the spread of communism.

9. The real enemy today is no longer communism but war itself.

10. We have no right to carry the struggle against communism to the point of risking the destruction of the human race.

2. The older women in both samples have the highest anti-nuclear scores.

3. Women's scores reflect a greater change in attitudes than men's.

4. The older men have the lowest anti-nuclear scores and show no change after viewing "The Day After."

Analysis of the scale's specific items revealed some unexpected changes in attitudes toward nuclear war, following the TV show. (Table A.3 in the Appendix shows the rank order of the ten items for the before and the after conditions, according to the degree of their anti-nuclear scoring).[3] Interestingly, specific items evoked consistently greater pro- or anti-nuclear responses across all groups and across the two populations. Thus, agreement with item 6—feeling relieved to know that some parts of the world would be spared, even if not ours—changed most dramatically down from its originally high anti-nuclear rank, after the TV viewing. Viewers seemed to become less altruistic and felt little consolation in knowing that some other part of the world might be spared. On the other hand, after the show, the responses to item 2—safety in missiles—indicated that respondents had become less confident that nuclear missiles in Europe lessen the danger to our own country.

Findings from the Questionnaire

The Nuclear War Questionnaire (see Figure 5.2) was devised to gain a further understanding of the attitudes that had triggered our research: people's apparent acceptance, apathy, and passivity regarding nuclear war issues. The general questions that prompted us were: Do people really believe that nuclear destruction is a possibility? Do they think about it? Can they grasp the consequences of such destruction? Can an awareness-raising event such as "The Day After" have an influence on views and actions?

We obtained responses to the questionnaires from 248 participants before viewing the TV show, and from 213 after the TV show. Since preliminary analysis of the data did not reveal significant differences between group responses, the age and gender groups were pooled for this part of the study (see Table A.4 in the Appendix). A summary of questionnaire responses follows. Interestingly, only questions 7, 8, and 10 elicited comments beyond the straight answer called for.

1. What is the probability of a nuclear war in your lifetime?

Among respondents questioned before the show, 84 percent believed nuclear war to be a definite possibility, while 12 percent believed that a nuclear war is either inevitable or impossible to occur.[4] These seemingly opposite responses are dynamically similar. Both believing that a nuclear war is an absolute certainty and

Figure 5.2
Nuclear War Questionnaire

```
                                      Age:          Sex:
                                      Profession:   Race:
```

1. What is the probability of a Nuclear War in your lifetime?

   1) inevitable
   2) Very likely (over 40%)
   3) Possible
   4) Impossible (0% chance)
   5) Other

2. How often do you think of the possibility of nuclear annihilation?

   1) Every day
   2) Often (once a week)
   3) Sometimes (maybe once a month)
   4) Hardly ever

3. What would a nuclear disaster be like?

   1) Limited damage to some regions
   2) Extinguish life on Earth
   3) Extinction of planet
   4) Other

4. If there are any survivors, what would your preference be?

   1) Be one of them, whatever the condition
   2) Survive, as long as you do not suffer physically
   3) Die at the moment of impact
   4) Die before the disaster occurs

5. Have you had dreams of apocalypses (i.e., earthquakes, planetary
   destruction, other mass death)? Yes _____ No _____

6. Can we avoid a nuclear war? Yes _____ No _____

7. Do nuclear weapons in your locale make you feel more, or less, safe?

   1) More safe_____ 2) Less safe _____
   3) If "less safe," where would you like to see them? _____

8. If the Soviets made a nuclear attack on one of our allies
   but will attack us only in self-defense, under which of the following
   casualty estimates would you, as president, order an attack?

   1) 100% of our population killed (200 million)   Yes____ No____
   2) 50%-75% killed (100-150 million)   Yes____ No____
   3) 10%-25% killed (20-50 million)   Yes____ No____
   4) Up to 1% killed (2 million or less)   Yes____ No____
   5) Other

9. How much of your energy are you willing to invest to help avoid nuclear
   disaster?

   1) None; there is nothing I can do; I feel utterly powerless
   2) Willing to make phone calls; write to representatives; talk to people
      about it
   3) Take part in demonstrations, even with threat of getting arrested
   4) Engage in civil disobedience; go to jail; risk getting beaten up
   5) I would not stop at anything, as long as I know I am helping to
      prevent nuclear war

10. Is death by nuclear annihilation more tragic to you than your eventual
    personal death (dying alone)?

    1) No_____ 2) Yes_____ Why?

believing that it has no chance at all have the same consequences as far as action is concerned. There is nothing one can do in the first instance, and nothing one needs do in the second.

Among those questioned after the show, 92 percent believed nuclear war to be possible, while only 5 percent persisted in considering nuclear war either inevitable or impossible.

2. How often do you think of the possibility of nuclear annihilation?

Before the show, the most frequent response was hardly ever, at 44 percent. This was followed closely by 34 percent who think of it sometimes (once a month). There were 10 percent who claimed to think often or daily about the threat of nuclear annihilation.

After the show, some obvious changes occurred in the frequency of thinking about nuclear war. Only 29 percent said that they hardly ever think about it; 42 percent responded sometimes; and 28 percent often or daily.

3. What would a nuclear disaster be like?

Before the show, 59 percent of the respondents viewed nuclear disaster as the extinction of life on Earth or even extinction of the planet, while 20 percent felt that the damage would be limited. (Another 20 percent mentioned other, usually more limited consequences.)

After the show, belief in the severity of a disaster increased, with 70 percent viewing it as extinction of life of the planet, and only 12 percent holding to their previous view of limited damage.

4. If there are any survivors, what would your preference be?

The most frequent alternative—chosen by 35 percent of the respondents—before the show was to survive as long as they do not suffer physically, followed by 31 percent choosing to die at the moment of impact. There were 17 percent who would prefer to die before the disaster occurs and 13 percent voiced a preference for survival, whatever the condition.

After the show, the order of survival preferences remained the same as before seeing "The Day After," but with some shifts in weight: 35 percent were still opting for survival as long as they do not suffer physically; 34 percent would choose to die at the moment of impact, and 22 percent before the disaster occurs. Only 9 percent would opt to survive whatever the condition.

5.   *Have you had dreams of apocalypses?*

Both before and after viewing the show, the vast majority of respondents (85 percent before, and 77 percent after) did not remember having had any such dreams.5

6.   *Can we avoid a nuclear war?*

No changes in views were observed after the TV show, with 86 percent of respondents both before and after believing that a nuclear war can be avoided.

7.   *Do nuclear weapons in your locale make you feel more, or less, safe?*

Before the show, 26 percent of respondents felt more safe with such weapons, while 68 percent felt less safe. A slight change in views occurred after the show, when 21 percent reported feeling safer and 71 percent said they feel less safe with nuclear weapons in their locale.

The same remarks were made before and after the show as to where respondents would like to see such weapons. Some of the most frequent answers were: nowhere; in remote (or isolated) areas; the desert; buried; on uninhabited islands; under the sea.

8.   *If the Soviets made a nuclear attack on one of our allies, but will attack us only in self-defense, under which of the following casualty estimates would you, as president, order an attack?*

Before the show, 70 percent of the respondents did not choose any of the casualty options, explaining that they would not order an attack. There were 14 percent willing to risk an attack with up to 2 million killed; 6 percent would risk 20–50 million lives; 3 percent would risk 100–150 million; and 7 percent would risk the entire population.

This question triggered an unexpected reaction in respondents after they viewed the TV show. The changes were in the direction of a greater pro-nuclear attitude: only 60 percent would refuse to order a nuclear attack; 19 percent chose the risk of up to 2 million killed; 9 percent would risk 20–50 million people; another 3 percent would risk 100–150 million killed; and 9 percent would order an attack at the risk of 100 percent of our population being killed.

> 9. *How much of your energy are you willing to invest to help avoid a nuclear disaster?*

Response to this question revealed an increase—from 33 percent to 41 percent—in willingness to invest some energy (phone calls, write to representatives, talk to people) after viewing the TV show. The original commitment of 21 percent of the respondents to large investments of energy and personal risk remained unchanged.

> 10. *Is death by nuclear annihilation more tragic to you than your eventual personal death?*

The attitudes expressed in response to this question—before as well as after the TV viewing—are perhaps the most disturbing ones: 28 percent of respondents before and 24 percent after did not consider death by nuclear annihilation more tragic than personal death. A number of respondents even favored death by nuclear annihilation over dying alone. The reasons given for their choices were frequently religious in nature and highly egocentric, lacking in perspective and imagination. Some of the most frequent comments were:

"Dying is dying."

"No [not more tragic]. Whatever way is least painful."

"No difference to me, if it's quick death."

"No. Death is finite. No degree or gradation on dying, no matter how it happens."

"We would all be together."

"No. I am ready to die, doesn't matter what kind of death."

"No matter how I die, I have a place in heaven."

"I don't want to die alone."

"If my time is up, I can't prevent death."

"How I die is no consequence to God, how I live is important."

"It's all God's will."

"It's in the Bible."

Those who favored personal (natural) death over nuclear annihilation expressed concern for the survival of their children, other family members, friends, life on Earth, our planet, and the continuation of culture (in that order). Some addressed themselves to the fact that personal death is a necessity one is more or less prepared for, while nuclear annihilation is avoidable.

Summary and Reflections

In seven of the eight groups of respondents, their quantitative as well as qualitative responses to the questionnaire and the attitude scale indicate a change in attitude in the direction of greater anti-nuclear views after viewing the TV show "The Day After." But inspection of the data of individual respondents also reveals that the show had the opposite effect on certain participants, who expressed an increase in pro-nuclear attitudes after the show. Furthermore, specific questions—such as item 6 on the attitude scale (feeling relieved to know that some would be spared), and item 8 on the questionnaire (ordering an attack based on casualty estimates)—triggered an increase in pro-nuclear attitudes across all groups, including women with their overall high anti-nuclear attitude.

The increased aggressiveness elicited by question 8 on ordering an attack and risking the death of millions can be understood as a reaction to the fear evoked by this film, within the cultural context of historically resolving conflict in aggressive, warlike modes. This increase in pro-nuclear attitudes may be explained further in terms of feelings of vulnerability and the need for self-protection when confronted with personal risk of annihilation and anger against the "enemy." LaFarge (1987) found that men in general have less tolerance for feelings of vulnerability than women do. Men socialized into traditional role stereotypes would therefore have a greater propensity to respond to that threat aggressively, acting out their perception of the realism of strength. This interpretation does not, however, explain the active role that women have played throughout the world in promoting peace and, in some instances, promoting war. These apparent contradictions are discussed further in Chapter 7, which analyzes the gender differences in cross-cultural responses.

An in-depth item analysis revealed some other unexpected findings. Individuals are not necessarily consistent in their responses. For instance, on the attitude scale we frequently find agreement with both item 8 (we must be willing to run the risk of nuclear war to prevent the spread of communism) and item 10 (we have no right to carry the struggle against communism to the point of risking destruction of the human race); or disagreement with item 4 (any consequence is better than the destruction of our planet) and agreement with item 5 (the survival of future generations is more important than the continuation of our form of government). These are contradictory choices. They may be due, in part, to a response bias toward or against the way an item was formulated, regardless of its meaning.

However, some of the remarks made in the interviews indicate that these items trigger feelings of ambivalence because of conflicting ideologies and perspectives. Thus, placing survival itself above any of the circumstances of living is often seen as demeaning to personal values and ideals (item 4), reflected also in the willingness of some to die for their values (or whatever one is opposed to). But the idea of condemning others to extinction for the sake of our own beliefs may be just as unacceptable (item 5). There is also the conflict between broad and narrow time perspectives. In trying to decide how much to agree or disagree on particular items, respondents often remarked on the disparity between their immediate and long-term preferences—referring to the limited duration of political systems as compared to the duration of our planet.

REVELATIONS OF THE OMNICIDAL PERSONALITY PATTERN

Despite the disparities and contradictions chronicled above, we found a startling relationship forming among the responses given by a large number of the interviewees—revealing the organized response pattern that we have come to call the "omnicidal personality." As noted earlier, this personality pattern is characterized especially by passivity, dependence, denial, and a fatalistic outlook regarding the future. Since the respondents' mode of reacting to the nuclear threat is of major importance to our present endeavor, we shall summarize the relevant features of omnicidal responses in the context of this study.

The response to the first questionnaire item is the most crucial one: if the probability of a nuclear war within their lifetime were seen either as inevitable or as impossible, then the prediction of respondents' other attitudes could be made with a fair amount of accuracy. However, omnicidal individuals do not necessarily choose one of the two extreme responses.

Since—realistically—a nuclear war can occur but does not necessarily have to occur, the opportunity exists for a denial of reality. Repression too is one of the hallmarks of an omnicidal orientation. Thus, not surprisingly, we find that many of our respondents hardly ever think about a nuclear disaster. And both repression and denial of reality are again manifested in the belief that a nuclear disaster would cause only limited damage to some regions.

Part of the omnicidal response syndrome is demonstrated by the quite frequent unwillingness to invest any energy in preventing a nuclear disaster, with feelings of inadequacy and powerlessness reflected in comments such as: nothing I can do about it; I have no control over it.

Some additional omnicidal response tendencies are the absence of remembering apocalyptic dreams, and the view of death by nuclear annihilation being no more tragic than personal death. The total serendipitous discovery of this omnicidal response syndrome led us to further studies of the omnicidal personality makeup, which we present in Chapter 6.

Finally, we need to address people's general response to "The Day After" and how their assessment of it is related to omnicidal personality traits. There was no consensus as to the positive or negative value of the show. In general, we found people highly critical of it, pointing just as frequently to shortcomings and weaknesses in the production as to its strength. Even those who hold strong anti-nuclear attitudes were critical of the show. Such general criticizing of the show may again reflect the use of defense mechanisms—a key factor in the omnicidal personality. As long as one can find fault with the technicalities of a production, one can deny the show's message and its realistic possibilities, and thus diminish its impact.

But the evaluation of the show in terms of its production flaws or its level of artistic excellence misses the true importance of the event. "The Day After" did to the topic of nuclear war what Freud had done to the topic of sex, and Kubler-Ross to the topic of death. It lifted the taboo on thinking and talking about nuclear war. It raised awareness and forced people to face the possibility of our totally annihilating life as we know it now.

But has the taboo been lifted for good? Has the film's effect been a lasting one? There are indications that it has. We administered the Nuclear Attitude Scale to students and to college administrators and faculty at several college meetings four and five months after the show. The effect may very well be an indirect one—some of the respondents may not have even seen the show—but the nuclear war theme is now part of the zeitgeist. Discussions, TV talk shows, documentaries, articles, workshops, and even newly devised college courses on the topic have mushroomed since the show was aired. As a matter of fact, the phrase "the day after" has become an idiom of expression, referring uniquely to nuclear war.

6

Omnicidal and Suicidal Personalities: A Comparison

From the very beginning of our investigations of the nuclear dilemma we have been most concerned by the apathy shown by the majority of people regarding the nuclear threat. Though the passive consent of millions of people will not by itself cause a nuclear holocaust, it may very well be a factor that contributes to triggering it. We need to find some way to reverse the now-prevalent passive acceptance into an active resistance against omnicide. Certainly, a better understanding of the omnicidal mind-set is necessary in any attempt to change it.

Desensitization to major catastrophes, and psychic numbing in general, have been discussed at length in the literature (see, for example, Lifton and Falk 1982). Somerville (1979, 1982) debunks the absurd notion of fighting and winning a nuclear war, by assigning to it a more accurate term: "nuclear omnicide." But the study of omnicidal attitudes and characteristics has been ignored by the major authors concerned with nuclear war issues.[1] As a matter of fact, omnicidal characteristics have been obscured by confounding them with suicidal characteristics. Thus, the passive acquiescence on the part of a large segment of the population to the possibility of human annihilation, together with the high potential for realizing it, has been commonly referred to as "mass suicide" or as an act of "national suicide" in recent war literature.

Indeed, if our species is threatened with extinction, it is not an external cataclysmic event that threatens us, but the possibility of humanity's annihilation at its own hand. Such self-destructive tendencies toward one's own species may well be taken for suicide, but not if omnicidal and suicidal behavior patterns are carefully distinguished.

Omnicidal personality patterns, as revealed in our research on attitudes toward nuclear war, seem at variance with the suicidal ones described in the voluminous suicidology literature and briefly summarized here for comparison purposes. In this book, we refer to those who are most accepting of or least resistant to the possibility of nuclear annihilation as "omnicidal." By "suicide," we mean a fatal act that is self-inflicted, *consciously* intended, and carried out with the knowledge that death is irreversible. The term "self-destructiveness" includes not only those who complete suicide, but also those who entertain thoughts of suicide, threaten suicide, or make suicide attempts (sometimes repeatedly) as well as those who gradually destroy themselves through substance abuse, neglect of medical regimens, or starvation (Hoff 1989: 190–92). In contrast to omnicidal tendencies, suicide or suicide attempts[2] are more circumscribed and usually occur in response to individual traumatic life events or circumstances. However, as discussed later, one's interpretation of these individual life events may be influenced by the pervasive threat of nuclear holocaust.

Three key ingredients of a suicidal person's behavior are *intentionality* (Shneidman 1985), the *desire for change*, and *activity* to bring about the change. Broadly speaking, the intentions of self-destructive persons fall into two categories of desired change: (1) from life to death; and (2) from a painful to a less painful quality of life. Depending on the degree of distress, the preference for death over life may be temporary or less than absolute. Usually this is expressed as ambivalence—the desire to live and die at the same time.

Among those with a history of emotional turmoil and suicidal disposition, there are other hallmarks: despair, hopelessness, an absence of perceived alternatives, inflexible thought patterns (sometimes referred to as "telescopic vision"), actual or perceived lack of social support, and often a fear of death and a fear of openness to try other options if sufficiently ambivalent about death. Finally, and very importantly, the suicidal person usually feels very powerless except for the supreme choice of death over life and the final action on that choice. Suicide, then, is one of the most powerful of individual actions, and its social and cultural meaning (Hoff 1989: 175–79 and 214–16)—especially among young people—is highly relevant to the theme of this book.

Of particular note throughout this description is the self-destructive person's *active* role in the complex process of bringing about her or his own death. This feature contrasts sharply with a dominant characteristic of omnicidal persons: their *passivity* in the face of possible extinction of themselves and the entire planet. Omnicidal personalities also appear to be far more monolithic than the various types of suicidal persons, and they outnumber the latter by four or five to one.3

By simplistically equating omnicide with suicide, the study of the omnicidal personality has been neglected. But just as suicide prevention demands an understanding of the dynamics of the suicidal person, so too the prevention of omnicide requires an understanding of the omnicidal personality. Though suicidal and omnicidal individuals share some of the same tendencies—such as strong dependency needs, and feelings of powerlessness—the context in which they occur and the way they are dealt with are very different. The suicidal individual is likely to use *reaction formation* as a defense against anxiety and feelings of powerlessness, thereby converting death from the most feared occurrence into a freely chosen, desired condition and thus taking control over life and death. The omnicidal person—on the other hand—uses *regression*, reverting to childhood patterns of behavior and relying on an authority figure to shoulder all responsibility. This is indicated by remarks such as: there is nothing I can do about it; it's not my responsibility; I'm just a little guy; I trust our president (or government) to do the right thing. In contrast, the suicidal person's feelings of powerlessness do *not* extend to the ultimate life-and-death decision, as reflected in power statements such as: I have the right to kill myself and you don't have the right to stop me.

To obtain a sharper differentiation between suicidal and omnicidal dispositions, and to gain a better understanding of the latter, we surveyed 242 U.S. citizens between the ages of 18 and 50. Our discussion here is limited to responses obtained to the target questions on a ten-item questionnaire dealing with nuclear threat and personal death (Goodman 1985; see Figure 6.1).

The last three questions on the list served as criteria for classifying respondents into one of three groups: suicidal, omnicidal, or survivor (those who are neither suicidal nor omnicidal). To be classified as *suicidal*, respondents had to indicate that the possibility of their life ending in suicide is very likely or almost certain. Furthermore, they must have seriously thought about committing suicide, or attempted suicide in the past.[4]

The *omnicidal* classification required that respondents indicate total support for their government—whatever its decision in questions concerning war or peace—and/or express feelings of utter powerlessness in having any influence over these questions. Those classified as *survivors* had indicated that it would be impossible or highly unlikely for their life to end by suicide; they had never considered suicide as a possibility; and finally, they would resist their government to the utmost should it lead the nation into nuclear war.[5]

According to these criteria, 64 participants fell into the suicidal category, 101 into the omnicidal, and 77 into the survivor category. However, 26 of those classified as suicidal possessed some of the omnicidal dispositions, as well—an interesting finding, especially in terms of the increasing incidence of youth suicide. (For the distribution of the sample population, see Table A.5 in the Appendix.) Our focal concern here is with respondents who were classified as either suicidal or omnicidal. (For a summary of certain critical responses to the differentiation questionnaire along with statistical data on differences between the two groups, see Table A.6 in the Appendix.)

Figure 6.1
Suicide/Omnicide Differentiation Questionnaire

1. HOW OFTEN DO YOU THINK ABOUT YOUR OWN DEATH?
   a. every day
   b. often (about once a week)
   c. sometimes (about once a month)
   d. hardly ever
   COMMENTS? (please make them on back of page)

2. HOW OFTEN DO YOU THINK OF THE POSSIBILITY OF NUCLEAR AN-
   NIHILATION?
   a. every day
   b. often (once a week)
   c. sometimes (once a month)
   d. hardly ever
   COMMENTS? (please make them on back of page)

3. WHAT IS THE PROBABILITY OF A NUCLEAR WAR IN YOUR
   LIFETIME?
   a. inevitable
   b. very likely (over 60%)
   c. fair possibility (about 50%)
   d. possible but unlikely
   e. impossible (0% chance)
   COMMENTS? (please make them on back of page)

4. HOW MUCH OF YOUR ENERGY ARE YOU WILLING TO INVEST TO HELP
   AVOID NUCLEAR DISASTER? (circle the most applicable ones)
   a. none: there is nothing I can do; I feel utterly
      powerless; other (circle correct ones)
   b. some: write to representatives; make phone calls;
      talk to people about it; other
   c. take part in demonstrations; risk getting arrested
   d. engage in civil disobedience; go to jail; risk
      getting beaten up
   e. all my energy. I would not stop at anything as long
      as I can help prevent a nuclear war

5. THE WORST THING ABOUT NUCLEAR WAR IS:
   a. it is not necessary (not like personal death); we
      can avoid it; our fault if it happens
   b. the suffering it would cause
   c. my feeling powerless; that there is nothing I can
      do about it
   d. other, explain:

6. WHAT DO YOU CONSIDER THE GREATEST TRAGEDY?
   a. your own death
   b. death of the person closest to you
   c. nuclear annihilation
   d. other, explain:

7. IS DEATH BY NUCLEAR ANNIHILATION MORE OR LESS TRAGIC TO
   YOU THEN YOUR EVENTUAL PERSONAL DEATH (DYING ALONE)?
   a. more tragic
   b. less tragic
   c. makes no difference to me
   COMMENTS? (please respond below)

8. WHEN IT COMES TO QUESTIONS OF WAR AND PEACE:
   a. I would support my government, whatever decisions
      it makes
   b. I feel utterly powerless in having any influence
      over it
   c. I would do all I can to resist our government
      leading us into a nuclear war
   d. If other, explain:

9. WHAT IS THE POSSIBILITY OF YOUR LIFE ENDING BY SUICIDE?
   a. impossible (whatever the conditions)
   b. very unlikely (less than 10% chance)
   c. possible (20% - 50% chance of happening)
   d. very likely (better than 50% chance)
   e. almost certain that my life will end by suicide
   COMMENTS: (please respond below)

10. DID YOU:
    a. ever think seriously about committing suicide?
    b. ever attempt to commit suicide?
    c. I never considered suicide as a possibility
    d. if other, explain

The defense mechanisms of repression and denial of reality are inferred from responses to the following three questions:

1. Question 1—How often do you think about your own death?
2. Question 2—How often do you think of the possibility of nuclear annihilation?
3. Question 3—What is the probability of a nuclear war in your lifetime?

The frequency of thinking about one's own death, as well as thinking about nuclear annihilation, is reported to a significantly higher degree by the suicidal than the omnicidal respondents— while almost twice as many omnicidal as suicidal respondents claim that they hardly ever think about their own death or about nuclear annihilation. The majority of individuals in the omnicidal group believe that nuclear war in their lifetime is unlikely or even impossible to occur, while suicidal group members' responses indicate far greater pessimism on this account.

Thus, our preliminary observations of repression and denial of reality as strongly developed omnicidal tendencies were borne out. Suicidal people—unlike omnicidal ones—while usually facing a grim reality in their personal worlds, do not deny this reality but instead take action against it. One may argue about the soundness of their turning anger and disappointment against themselves; nevertheless, their action contrasts with the passivity following on denial that characterizes omnicidal people.

Dimensions of control or power were inferred from the specific alternative chosen in response to the following two questions.

*Question 4   How much of your energy are you will-
ing to invest to help avoid nuclear disaster? (circle
the most applicable ones)*

a. none: there is nothing I can do; I feel utterly powerless; other (circle correct one(s))

b. some: write to representatives; make phone calls; talk to people about it; other

c. take part in demonstrations; risk getting arrested

d. engage in civil disobedience; go to jail; risk getting beaten up

e. all my energy. I would not stop at anything as long as I can help prevent a nuclear war

In the omnicidal group, 36 percent of the respondents indicated that they would not invest any energy, feeling utterly powerless— compared to only 5 percent of suicidal respondents who feel the same way.

Question 5   The worst thing about nuclear war is:

a. it is not necessary; we could avoid it; (our fault if it happens)

b. the suffering it would cause

c. my feeling powerless; nothing I can do about it

d. other, explain

Though the first alternative was most frequently chosen by all groups, there were three times more omnicidal than suicidal respondents who chose "feeling powerlessness" as the worst aspect.

Dependency needs as well as a lack of imagination may be inferred from responses to the next question.

Question 6   What do you consider the greatest tragedy?

a. your own death

b. death of the person closest to you

c. nuclear annihilation

d. other, explain

While nuclear annihilation is seen as the greatest tragedy by half of the suicidal individuals, the majority of the omnicidal group members feel that the death of the person closest to them would be most tragic.

The reaction of both the omnicidal and the suicidal respondents to Question 7 is rather disturbing: 48 percent of omnicidal and 30 percent of suicidal respondents do not view death by nuclear destruction as more tragic than their eventual personal death. Only 12 percent of the survivor group share that view. This apparent indifference or apathy toward the fate of our world demonstrates a mind-set totally absorbed with narrow self-interest, and most likely also a lack of imagination.

The findings of this survey are consistent with our previous observations of the omnicidal personality makeup. Our research suggests that adverse or fear-producing aspects of reality are repressed or denied by omnicidal individuals. Anti-introspection is another way they deal with, or rather avoid dealing with, anxiety-arousing problems. These omnicidal strategies—namely, distortion of reality and self-deception, seen in denial and repression—make for a more optimistic view of the world than the one held by suicidal individuals.

Furthermore, omnicidal people are likely to have a vast support system, since they belong to a large segment of the population that shares a similar mind-set. But the most fundamental difference between suicidal and omnicidal people lies in their active as against passive self-destructive behavior patterns. Remembering the sheep syndrome described in Chapter 3, we might say that those with omnicidal tendencies will get drowned for all their passivity. They are too lethargic or unequipped to move themselves and their contemporaries to higher ground. People who have a suicidal tendency differ in that they play an active part in the self-destructive process. They won't wait around until the water gets too high, but instead jump right into the flood.

Yet—as already suggested—in spite of the differences we have observed between suicidal and omnicidal persons, there are also similarities that may lie at the root of their destructive patterns and may clarify why some people in our sample possess both tendencies. Thus, alienation, egoism, a narrow time perspective, and lack of involvement or commitment are reflected in both suicidal and omnicidal persons. We explore these here with particular reference to contemporary increases in youth suicide, substance abuse, and concerns about the materialistic outlook of many in today's society.

A century ago, in his classic study of suicide, Emile Durkheim categorized suicidal persons as "anomic" and "egoistic" (along with "altruistic"). His classification evokes reference to our discussion about alienation, despair, and disengagement—among the young, particularly. Anomie as an explanation for suicide encompasses the notion of a person who at one time felt socially integrated, but now feels abandoned by social network members from whom she or he might have sought support. The concept of egoism suggests that the person was never well integrated into a social group in the first place, with the consequence that everything revolves in excess around the self, the ego. Durkheim's *social* interpretation of suicide represents only part of the picture, however. First of all, it shortchanges the power of *individual* factors contributing to suicidal behavior. And second, it does not account for the *interactional* relationship operating between the suicidal individual and familial and societal factors. It is precisely in the interactional realm that—we believe—lies the connection between the threat of nuclear holocaust and the increase in youth suicide, drug abuse, crime, and violence in general. It may also be here that suicidal and omnicidal tendencies exist together.

We do not propose a simple cause-and-effect relationship between nuclear threat and increased youth suicide and disengagement. Suicide—as we have said—is an individual act that ordinarily occurs in response to identifiable, concrete, painful circumstances. But these personally painful circumstances do not exist in a cultural vacuum. In a society like the United States where individual effort is so prized and where everyone is told that such effort will be rewarded, though real differences in opportunity persist, there is enormous potential for personal disappointment—whether in getting a good job, acquiring consumer goods, or generally (as they say) making it. Add to this the fact that many young people endure sexual or other abuse from family members, or observe the violence and substance abuse practiced by their parents, during the critical transition period of adolescence—which is already stressful enough.

Even the fortunate youth from "well-off" families (recall our treatment of this distinction in Chapter 4) routinely face other hazardous and unfamiliar events like the breakup of an important relationship, failure in school, changing sex roles, or the divorce of parents. The young person then—enduring this generally stressful life stage, facing some immediate disappointment, and lacking social support—now has a ready-made excuse for not struggling harder to overcome any of these odds: What's the use anyway, when the whole world may be blown up before I even get started.[6]

Thus, perhaps the young person may commit suicide, or escape into drugs and violence, not because of the nuclear threat per se. Rather, the nuclear threat creates a context—a featureless climate—in which self-destructive forms of behavior such as suicide or substance abuse become a convenient response to whatever the personally troubling circumstances happen to be. The rash of youth suicides sends a message that goes deeper than the personal depression of suicidal youth. Our young people seem to be telling us that they are not interested in remaining in the world we have created for them, and that there is no real chance for them to create an alternative and more desirable one. The climate of despair fostered by the nuclear threat seems to us analogous to the relationship between individual violence and the aggressive posture spawned by nuclearism and war. That is, socially approved violence like war creates a climate in which it is easy for individuals to justify a violent approach to individual stress reduction and interpersonal conflict resolution. In short, individual and interpersonal factors intersect with the societal factor of nuclear threat to produce both suicidal and omnicidal tendencies in individuals whose survival tactics against either suicide or nuclear threat do not work.

In Chapter 4 we discussed the gradual development of omnicidal personality characteristics, which were ascribed in part to an increase in feelings of powerlessness and a decrease in the rich imagination of childhood—with repression building up as a defense against this newly experienced vulnerability. We also suggested that the impact of futurelessness created by nuclear threat on individuals can be mitigated at the family and community levels. But we certainly cannot expose children to nuclear realities without replacing their deceptive defense structure with truthful, confidence-inspiring demonstrations of our own work toward a secure future. Thus, we cannot change children's attitudes—nor will we likely reduce the rates of youth suicide—without first changing the attitudes of adults. Strategies to effect such changes will be explored in Part III.

First, however, let us make a cross-cultural examination to discover its insights into current attitudes toward the nuclear threat.

7

Cross-cultural Differences in Attitudes toward Nuclear War

With a scenario of "mutual assured destruction" in case of a nuclear war, the fate of the inhabitants of our planet would be very much the same—no matter where they might be dwelling. However, the way we experience the nuclear dilemma will depend greatly on our environment and—most importantly—on the nation in which we live. The United States and the Soviet Union are the only countries that have the capacity to destroy our entire world. Thus, the responsibility, and with it the burden, on the citizens of these two countries far outweigh that among people in any other country. Though it seems that most of us feel powerless over the decisions of war and peace, we can at least nourish the hope that our own government in its decision-making position will act in accordance with our wishes.

But what is the attitude of the people who sit between the two superpowers and who not only feel powerless as individuals, but whose governments too have very little control over the triggering or the preventing of a nuclear holocaust? Is our experience different from theirs? Who faces the more disturbing dilemma?

We are reminded of the "executive rat" experiment: two rats are placed on an electrifiable grid, with shock delivered after a warning signal; the shock can be avoided by pressing a lever at the moment the signal appears. Both rats have learned the avoidance response, but only one of them is in position to press the lever. The rat in charge is therefore responsible for both of them either receiving the painful shock or avoiding it. Thus, one is the sitting duck—or rather, the sitting rat—and the other, the executive rat. After a few weeks, one of them develops ulcers. The question is, which one? Invariably, the executive rat! We cannot draw a direct analogy between the inhabitants of the superpowers as the executive rats and the people of all other countries as the sitting rats, without committing the ratamorphic fallacy; but we do expect a country's degree of nuclear potential to affect its people's attitudes toward the nuclear threat.

Included in our research on attitudes toward nuclear war is a cross-cultural project that will remain ongoing for years to come. The Nuclear War Questionnaire and the Nuclear Attitude Scale designed for the study reported in Chapter 5 seemed an appropriate instrument for an attitude assessment of Western Europeans, with some adaptation to other cultural settings. We therefore changed selected items and translated the instruments into Dutch, Spanish, French, and German. Thus far they have been administered to 100 French and 100 German participants surveyed between 1986 and 1988. We report here some of the highlights of our preliminary findings, with an emphasis on qualitative interpretation of the respondents' reactions to the questions.

THE GERMAN REACTION

From our past experience in attitude assessment in the United States, we took for granted that—after being briefed about the survey and expressing their willingness to take part—the participants would then proceed with the task in an orderly fashion, going from the first questionnaire item to the last. Not so in Germany! To begin with, most of our German participants first read through the entire questionnaire—a procedure that was frequently followed by criticism about the way the questions are "slanted." At this point, there was an occasional refusal to take part in the survey.

Almost all of the criticism was based on one of two opposite grounds: the questionnaires were perceived as having been devised by "Reaganite" reactionaries for the sake of obtaining distorted pro-defense statistics; or they were viewed as devised by "communists" in an attempt to show a lack of support in NATO alliances and to weaken U.S. security. In either case, there was suspicion that the survey was being used for political purposes.[1]

The objections of those who perceived a Reaganite influence were most frequently raised by the more radical students at the University of West Berlin; those perceiving a communist influence came primarily from older (over 50) male executives and professionals in the area of Stuttgart. Recruitment of this group was the most difficult.

Having one's attitude assessed was not taken at all lightly here, as can be observed by even a glance at the filled-out questionnaires: remarks are entered into all the spaces provided for comments; margins and in between the lines are seeded with explanations, lectures to the authors, and corrections; and even whole phrases in the questionnaires are crossed out or changed.[2]

The comments section was used much more liberally by the Germans than by the U.S. and French respondents for statements such as:

"It is frustrating to have to choose between unacceptable alternatives, which implies acceptance of the monstrous premise, a nuclear confrontation."

"I do not like your questions; they are suggestive and give 'false' alternatives."

The Germans' spirited reaction to the survey instrument may be colored by the historical fact that Germans have less reason to take their national security for granted than many U.S. citizens. Their direct experience with the effects of war is much more immediate than that of the majority of Americans. But in spite of the Germans' criticisms, they nevertheless revealed important information about their attitudes regarding the nuclear threat.

Our adaptation of the instrument focused on two items (2 and 7) of the attitude scale (see Figure 5.1) that were not considered appropriate for an assessment of attitudes other than in the United States. In the German scales, item 2 states, If nuclear missiles are deployed in NATO countries, the danger to my own country is lessened. Item 7 reads, In this dangerous world, it would be in our best interest to maintain utter neutrality.

Germans score consistently higher on anti-nuclear attitudes—as measured by the Nuclear Attitude Scales— than any other people we have surveyed in the United States or abroad. These considerably higher anti-nuclear scores held for each of the four groups when divided by sex and age (15–34 years; 35–70 years), as well as in the overall score.

However, there are some differences between the group scores that are primarily gender based, with the two female groups reflecting considerably higher anti-nuclear attitudes than those of the two male groups. (We discuss this finding later in concert with similar results from the French respondents). However, there are also age-based differences, with the greatest pro-nuclear attitudes reflected in the scores of the older male group.

There is remarkable agreement between and within groups on all but two items—the only two that evoke as many pro- as anti-nuclear responses: about half of the participants do not agree that in case of a nuclear war they would feel relieved to know that part of the world would be spared, even if theirs is destroyed (item 6). And only half of the interviewees favor—for the sake of safety—Germany taking a neutral stance (adapted item 7). With the exception of 43 percent of the older male group, Germans are almost unanimous in feeling that deployment of nuclear warheads in NATO countries does not enhance their safety.

In our European-adapted questionnaire (see Figure 5.2), we eliminated question 8, which dealt with the percentage of U.S. casualties a respondent would be willing to risk in order to retaliate against a Soviet attack on one of our allies. For this item, we substituted a question on the country Europeans perceived as presenting the greatest danger of starting a nuclear war: the United States, the Soviet Union, or an "other" country.

The most frequently occurring response (40 percent) to this question fingered both the United States and the Soviet Union as being equally dangerous. But 31 percent of respondents viewed the United States as most dangerous, while only 8 percent saw the Soviet Union in the same light. The remaining 20 percent of respondents mentioned other countries, usually with reference to the Middle East.

Our latest U.S. survey[3] reveals a startling reversal to the German viewpoint: only 8 percent of the U.S. interviewees consider their own country as most dangerous, while 22 percent view the Soviet Union as presenting the greatest danger in triggering a nuclear war. However, in the United States—similar to the response in Germany—both superpowers are seen as equally dangerous by 39 percent of respondents, while a substantial 31 percent point to Third World countries as most likely to start a nuclear war.

Question 1 deals with the probability of nuclear war occurring within the respondents' lifetime. Though the vast majority of Germans do not rule it out, only 15 percent believe such an occurrence to be inevitable or very likely. In this respect, their views are similar to those we have observed in the U.S. samples. But Germans indicate far greater preoccupation with the nuclear threat (question 2): 27 percent claim that they think very frequently about it (that is, daily or more than once a week), while only 26 percent claim that they hardly ever think about it. In contrast, the latter is the most frequent response in the United States: 48 percent of the U.S. respondents in 1987 say that they hardly ever think about it, while only 19 percent indicate that they think very frequently about the nuclear threat.

In addition to general gender-based differences, there are also remarkable gender differences in the German sample regarding preoccupation with nuclear threat. Thus, 40 percent of the male respondents deny any such preoccupation, compared to only 14 percent of the female respondents who make the same claim. Most

Germans are in agreement as to the consequences of a nuclear disaster (question 3): extinction of all life on earth or even extinction of the planet. The only exception to this response is the more than half of the older male group who say that such a disaster would cause only limited damage in some regions. Since there is no reason for us to believe that the over-35 German man is differently or less well informed about the consequences of a nuclear war than any of his compatriots, the "limited damage theory" must be a clear example of denial of reality. We should also note that no one in the older male group could remember ever having had an apocalyptic dream (question 5), though 21 percent of the women did remember such dreams.

Germans are just as optimistic as Americans in their belief that a nuclear war can be avoided (question 6). The majority of Germans and the majority of Americans (63 percent and 65 percent, respectively) say that the deployment of nuclear weapons in their area makes them feel less safe (question 7). But only 6 percent of Germans compared to 25 percent of Americans maintain that such deployment enhances their feeling of security. The remaining one-third of German respondents feel that such weapons in their locale neither add nor subtract from their security feelings.

In sharp contrast to U.S. participants, 57 percent of our German respondents declared their willingness to make a large investment of energy and to take great personal risks to help prevent nuclear war (question 9), while 29 percent would not invest any energy since they feel utterly powerless to have any effect. In the far more apathetic response of U.S. participants, only 15 percent say that they would be willing to make great energy investments and take personal risks, while 48 percent would decline any energy investment—claiming helplessness and powerlessness.

Question 10 requires the respondents to choose which of two alternatives they consider to be more tragic: death through nuclear annihilation, or eventual personal death. The German reactions to this question are as disturbing as those we encountered earlier in research conducted in the United States. Among the German respondents, 25 percent did not feel that death as a consequence of nuclear annihilation was any more tragic than one's natural personal death. And the reasons given were just as egocentric and as void of perspective and imagination as those of U.S. participants, although they lacked the religious references so frequently encountered in the U.S. samples. Below are some of the German comments made after indicating a preference not to die alone:

> "Because I hope it [death by nuclear annihilation] will go a lot faster."

> "Death for me is all the same: DEATH."

> "When I am dead I am dead. Only the survivors have to bear the consequences of a nuclear war."

> "All the same for me, as long as it is fast."

> "Both kinds of death are too abstract for me to answer the question."

> "To die in spite of or with the help of medication and medicine is just as horrible."

The comments of those who view death by nuclear annihilation as more tragic than their personal death revolve around a few common themes:

1. That personal death is a natural death, and therefore better;

2. A need to make preparations for one's death;

3. It being an outrage to die because of politics, greed, and stupidity of other people;

4. The fact that nuclear annihilation—unlike personal death—can be prevented;

5. That it represents the end of all life, the end of civilization; and

6. That it would take all meaning out of the life one has lived.

A 43-year-old nurse wrote,

I must die. I know that and I accept it. But it enrages me to think that I may have to die as a consequence of the madness, the arrogance, the stupidity, the brutality of people who hold themselves as being the most civilized, the wisest, the most Christian people on this planet.

A 19-year-old student wrote,

Nuclear death would signify the defeat of love for all the living. Perhaps we, the people, deserve it; after all we did it ourselves and to others, but "mother earth" does not deserve it. . . . Personally, I do not fear any kind of death, but I don't see myself only as an individual but also as part of humanity, and as such I fear nuclear annihilation more.

Returning to our sitting rat versus executive rat analogy, we do find differences between the Germans' and Americans' reactions to nuclear threat; but it does not seem that, under the burden of greater responsibility, Americans are more actively engaged in a search for solutions. To the contrary, the omnicidal tendencies of apathy, inactivity, and feelings of powerlessness along with their concomitant defenses of repression and denial of reality—so prominently displayed in the surveys conducted in the United States—do not seem characteristic among our German respondents. Thus, Germans report a far greater preoccupation with the nuclear issue (greater frequency in thinking about it), which indicates a lesser reliance on repression and denial as a defense against nuclear anxiety. They are also more likely than Americans to declare their willingness to invest energy and take personal risks in the struggle against nuclear war. This contrasts sharply with the apathy or passivity displayed by the U.S. respondents, who express a sense of futility about making any energy commitment since they view themselves as powerless.

Interestingly, we encountered "nuclearism" (Lifton and Falk 1982)—a form of worship of nuclear weapons, expressed by the creed of feeling safer when surrounded by them—in 25 percent of the U.S. respondents, while only 6 percent of the Germans surveyed feel that their safety is enhanced by the presence of nuclear arms. The embracing of nuclearism can be interpreted as a reaction formation—an anxiety-reducing defense mechanism that transforms a feared object (nuclear arms) into a desirable one. Furthermore, by making allies of powerful nuclear arms, a person's own feelings of inadequacy and powerlessness can be denied.

Reading through the comments in the margins of the German records can give one a very strong impression of the more qualitative, emotionally charged flavor in their attitudes toward the nuclear threat. The comments reveal many subtle forms of anger, frustration, and hostility—rather than omnicidal tendencies such as complacency and resignation. The following examples will have to suffice as a few cases in point.

Question 7 in the latest surveys reads, Do nuclear weapons in your locale make you feel: (1) more safe; (2) less safe; (3) neither more nor less safe; (4) if less safe, where would you like to see them? The majority responded with just one word: "nowhere." A few did elaborate, however, with remarks such as:

"I see such systems as purely offensive weapons and I am against their deployment anywhere in the world."

"If at all, then only in the USA."

"Who would want to be a target (or battleground) for the protection of America and Russia?"

In contrast, Americans usually leave the fourth option blank, or else they suggest unpopulated areas such as in the sea, on the moon, in the desert, or on deserted islands. Occasionally they too want to see the weapons "nowhere."

Question 8 asks which country (the United States, the Soviet Union, or other) presents the greatest danger in starting a nuclear war. Among the Germans, this triggered remarks such as:

"America and its satellites."

"It is not a question of "most dangerous country," but rather of the personality of the people in government; they often differ very little from each other."

One person crossed out all three given options, and replaced the country names with "humans"—the greatest danger.

On the attitude scale, we found several of the German records with the last half of item 9 crossed out and reworded to read, The real enemy today is capitalism, which leads to wars—or some variation of this sentiment—in place of the original statement, The real enemy is no longer communism but war itself.

Perhaps one could argue that the citizens of a country like the United States—with a powerful government that can wield the fate of the earth—feel a very great discrepancy between their own lack of control and the control in the hands of their government. The perception of such disparity between personal and governmental power may increase citizens' feelings of being powerless to influence the most vital decisions. In contrast, the citizens of a country that has been largely at the mercy of decisions made by other countries may feel much more powerful to exert influence on their own government. Furthermore, they can relieve anxiety by projecting all that is threatening and evil in the world to an outside force: the United States, the Soviet Union, or the Middle East perhaps.

Recalling the beginning of this particular survey, we had noted the circumspect way in which the Germans approached the task of filling out our questionnaires. They distrusted the motives of the investigators; they were suspicious about how the information would be used; their many comments indicate apprehension of being misinterpreted. One could say that such responses look like a paranoid reaction, which is closely related to projection as a mechanism of defense. The blame for the threatening world situation in which we all live must be projected to an outside source in order to demonstrate one's own innocence. One could even conjecture that the mechanism of projection is a deeply ingrained characteristic here, calling for a scapegoat whenever situations arise that are viewed as life threatening to oneself and to national security. In another interpretation, the Germans' heightened concern about the threat of nuclear war is based in the reality of their recent history and experience of war and their vulnerability in local and regional conflict situations.

THE FRENCH REACTION

The French approach to the survey is one of detachment and nonchalance. There were numerous out-of-hand refusals to take part in the survey, coming most frequently from the older male population.[4] Written comments are rare, even in spaces where they are specifically requested.

However, the French do not hesitate to express their views freely in the personal interviews we conducted in conjunction with the survey. The items and questions are identical to those used in the German survey, with the exception of item 7 on the attitude scale—where the original item was used (see Figure 5.1). The French score higher on anti-nuclear attitudes (as measured by our attitude scale) than the U.S. respondents, but far lower than the Germans. However, these differences hold only for the overall scores (the mean or average score of all participants), and not for specific groups when divided by age and sex.

In fact, the differences in attitudes here are strictly gender based, with scores of women in both the younger and the older group reflecting far greater anti-nuclear attitudes than those of men. Women in both age groups obtained almost identical attitude scores, and so did the older and younger male groups. The gender differences that have emerged in our attitude assessments of every culture we have surveyed thus far may perhaps be explainable along the lines of our Chapter 1 discussion of aggression being a consequence of child-rearing practices (and further elaborated in Chapter 9).

Aside from gender differences, there is very little homogeneity between as well as within French groups in reaction to individual items. We even have some examples of pro-nuclear choices, which are almost nonexistent in the German and U.S. protocols (other than in records of older men). Thus, for 41 percent of French respondents, nuclear annihilation is an abstract concept with no basis in reality (item 1). More than half of the respondents feel their country to be in less danger as long as there are nuclear missiles deployed in NATO countries (item 2). Some 17 percent would even prefer to run the risk of nuclear war and the destruction of our planet to the spread of communism (item 8). And a high 44 percent feel that the best strategy is to have first-strike capacity (item 7).

Responses to the questionnaire indicated that the French—old as well as young; women as well as men—are far less concerned with the nuclear dilemma than the Americans or the Germans are. For instance, 30 percent of the French respondents view a nuclear war in their lifetime as being a highly unlikely, if not impossible, occurrence (question 1). Note the far more pessimistic view held by Germans and Americans, discussed in the previous section. Among our French respondents, 61 percent claim that they hardly ever think about nuclear annihilation (question 2), while only 4 percent say that they think about it frequently (more than once a week). The impact of such a disaster—should it ever occur—is also seen as less devastating, with 29 percent imagining that damage would be limited to only a few regions (question 3).

There are also indications of nuclearism—similar to what we have encountered in the United States—with 27 percent of the French respondents claiming to feel greater safety with nuclear arms in their region (question 7). Only 6 percent of Germans hold the same view. In contrast to the German respondents, the French view the Soviet Union as the most likely country to initiate a nuclear war (question 8): 36 percent hold that view, while only 11 percent see the United States as the most dangerous country; 24 percent point to both the United States and the Soviet Union as equally dangerous, while 24 percent fear Third World countries most.

Contrary to their German counterparts, there is little commitment among the French to invest their personal energy into the prevention of nuclear war (question 9): 40 percent respond that they would not invest any energy, and only 22 percent of the respondents claim that they would be willing to invest a great deal of energy. The French we surveyed seem to be even less altruistic than either the Americans or the Germans: 39 percent of them do not conceive of death as a consequence of nuclear annihilation to be any more tragic than their own personal death (question 10).

Though—overall—the French responses resemble the omnicidal reactions obtained in the United States, they cannot be explained along the same lines. For one thing, no consistent pattern such as the omnicidal response syndrome can be detected in the individual records. Thus, when a French respondent holds the view that the occurrence of nuclear war in her or his lifetime is impossible, one cannot predict with any amount of confidence that the same person will also claim to: (1) hardly ever think about it; (2) subscribe to the limited damage theory; and (3) be unwilling to make any energy investment to help prevent nuclear war. And none of the occasional remarks on the records or made during the personal interviews reflect feelings of powerlessness or inadequacy.

Interestingly, apocalyptic dreams are more often remembered here than either in Germany or the United States—especially by younger women, with 36 percent of that group reporting such dreams (question 5). The lack of any consistent pattern within individual records makes the French participants appear more complex, or perhaps just more contradictory, than most other people we have surveyed thus far.

Though the French seem to be generally less pessimistic about the fate of our planet, we do not think that optimism and pessimism are national characteristics. Rather, we ascribe these general attitudes to the meaning that specific concepts acquire in different contexts, and to the needs created by the different environments and our interpretation of these environments.

For one thing, "nuclear energy"—in whatever form it occurs—has a different connotation in France than it has in Germany, the United States, and the Soviet Union. France relies on nuclear power for most of her energy needs, and in fact leads the world in reliance on nuclear power. Demonstrations against nuclear power plants are unheard of here. The French seem to have succeeded in convincing themselves that nuclear energy is a positive asset. We can speculate that this might change if and when the French ever experience a nuclear plant accident such as at Three Mile Island, or when waste from aging nuclear weapons plants threaten the health of surrounding residents as is currently happening in the United States.[5] Another factor influencing the French is the fact that they have their own nuclear arsenal. This has at least the psychological effect of freeing them from feeling utterly at the mercy of the United States or the Soviet Union.

Actually, the French attitudes that came across in the personal interviews presented a much more unified image than the rather contradictory one gained from the questionnaires. What seems to affect their views most profoundly is their sense of themselves and of their country. There is a major inconsistency here between the cognitive and the affective components of the French people's attitude toward the role of France in the world. Intellectually they know that France is not a major world power, but emotionally they live under the illusion that it is yet such a power. The French do not seem to feel that they are at the mercy of any foreign power, but rather that they are militarily independent. This accounts at least in part for their military withdrawal from the NATO alliance and the removal of the NATO headquarters from Paris to Brussels. The French like to entertain the pretense that their concurrence is needed on any far-reaching action the superpowers might think to promulgate. France's powerful-nation status rests in the mind or the make-believe of the French people, rather than in their government.

Perhaps the inconsistencies between the feeling and the thinking parts in some of their attitudes can account for the apparently contradictory responses we encountered. One is tempted to generalize that—where Americans rely primarily on repression and denial of reality, and the Germans on projection—the French use rationalization as a defense against nuclear anxiety.

III

Where Do We Go from Here?

8

A Future without Nuclear Threat

Up to this point, our discussion of the nuclear dilemma has proceeded on safe grounds. We reached back into the past, describing phenomena we deemed relevant to our present situation; and we reported research findings that shed some light on people's frame of reference, their present-day attitudes, their mind-set. However, we did not undertake all these studies to confine ourselves simply to reporting our findings. From the very beginning it has been our hope that, by living for years with the devastating nuclear threat and questioning people openly and directly on the subject, we might gain a better understanding of our dilemma, brought about at least in part by apathetic people—populations with omnicidal personality patterns—who seem incapable of resisting the possibility of their own destruction. We hoped that the deeper insight gained from these studies would bring us a step closer to a future without nuclear threat. Thus, we have reached the point where we must take the leap into the future; we must ask the question, where do we go from here?

CHANGE VERSUS MAINTAINING THE STATUS QUO

Projection into the future is a risky business. Generally, people harbor a deep distrust for tackling anything without precedent. Confronting a known entity—however frightening—is less anxiety provoking than facing the unknown. *Description* of what is has always been the ideal paradigm for serious study—not *prescription* for change. This has been one of the major difficulties confronting any serious discussion and warning about the perils of nuclear confrontation. The fact that we cannot look back to a worldwide nuclear holocaust—the fact that we have never experienced it—allows those interested in continuing the arms race to equate creative thinkers—those concerned commentators who are capable of a few deductive leaps—with soothsayers.

Under the pretext that only "value free," "objective" knowledge—arrived at by description and deduction from observed phenomena—is the legitimate paradigm for predicting future events, the nuclearists reject any warnings of likely cataclysmic events. Thus, Donald P. Snow, former secretary of the navy senior research fellow at the U.S. Naval War College, has espoused the thesis that nuclear weapons have a stabilizing and tranquilizing effect on U.S.–Soviet relationships. He writes that

> the major problem with the nuclear winter hypothesis is that it is just that—a hypothesis. The phenomena and dynamics associated with the nuclear winter have never been systematically observed and recorded. (Snow 1987: 128)

And quoting Carrier, Snow continues:

> There is little doubt that atmospheric modifications . . . would occur. But their extent and duration—and hence their potential impact on people, food supplies, and other biological systems—are very difficult to determine, and they remain controversial. (Carrier 1985, quoted in Snow 1987: 128)

Snow concludes that the peace imposed by nuclear weaponry works. Not only does it work, but he finds that there is

> little indication of basic malaise that requires alteration. Until there is stronger evidence that the system is failing, it falls

upon the reformers to demonstrate that their innovations represent positive change. (Snow 1987: 128)

As long as we ignore some 150 declared and undeclared wars since the end of World War II—which have caused 25 million fatalities—Snow is safe in his challenge to the "reformers." As long as we ignore the possibility of nuclear accidents, and as long as governments worldwide continue enormous defense expenditures instead of attending to global environmental and domestic crises, Snow is safe in his challenge. But if we need to wait until our military and environmental systems really fall apart or catastrophically fail, if we need to wait for still another Three Mile Island or Chernobyl, then his challenge is unconscionable and can no longer be met.

Snow's assurances that our nuclear weapons policy has worked, and that there is no malaise, reflects the same strategy our government and the military–industrial complex has used to avoid any consciousness raising and any increased participation of the public in policymaking decisions—which might interfere with the continuation of the arms race. We are reminded of the reassuring tone of the government officials addressing the survivors in the TV show "The Day After." The strength of this strategy was reaffirmed in the 1988 election: how quickly a presidential candidate who challenged the status quo in nuclear policy could be eliminated on the carefully orchestrated impression—widely accepted by the voting majority—of his being "weak on defense"!

But how realistic is a defense policy that contradicts all the experts who say there is no safe defense—not even in the stars? How realistic or honest is a policy that conceals how much nuclear defense systems really cost us in terms of society's neglected domestic needs (Gralnick 1988: 181)? And what about the absence of malaise that Snow claims? Our own research reveals a high incidence of omnicidal personalities and a malaise that has replaced pathological dimensions. Our respondents clearly testify to a keen awareness of feeling powerless, shown also in their apathetic reactions and the use of defenses such as repression and denial of reality. These reactions certainly do not suggest peace of mind.

But how can we propose solutions to our nuclear dilemma if such proposals demand we alarm people to events that have not yet taken place? How can we counteract the popularity of the "optimists" who are interested in maintaining the status quo, and who refer to those intending to eradicate omnicidal threat as "doomsayers"?

Robert J. Lifton has attempted to use Hiroshima as our "text." He writes,

> I spoke of Hiroshima together with Nagasaki, as a last chance, a nuclear catastrophe from which one could still learn. The bomb had been dropped, there was an "end of the world" in ways we have observed, yet the world still exists. And precisely in this end-of-the-world quality of Hiroshima lies both its threat and its potential wisdom. (Lifton and Falk 1982: 44–45)

Lifton goes on to point out the lessons that must be learned from Hiroshima: "the important nuclear age truths. . . . The first of these is the *totality of destruction*" (p. 5, emphasis his). At the same time, he warns of the inadequacy of Hiroshima as our *only* text:

> We know well that what happened there could not really represent what would happen to people if our contemporary nuclear warheads were used. . . . The scale of Hiroshima was difficult enough to grasp; now the scale is again so radically altered that holding literally to Hiroshima images misleads us in the direction of extreme understatement. (p. 45)

It seems to us that we can rely on our interpolative abilities—not to speak of our best scientists' deductions—to imagine what would happen if our present warheads were used. There are now approximately 60,000 nuclear warheads of 71 different types, intended for 116 weapons systems (Bethe 1985). Some of these warheads are 100 or 1,000 or more times the destructive power of those first two "tiny" bombs dropped on Hiroshima and Nagasaki—the only two atomic weapons in existence in the world at that time.

Yet there are still some people around who embrace nuclearism and try to convince us that we can survive a nuclear war, as long as we have "enough shovels" to dig a hole deep enough for us to stand in.[1] But the rhetoric of a "winnable nuclear war" has cooled in response to public polls that show people's intolerance for upping the ante, in contrast to favoring détente. It was precisely such public intolerance that led to the freeze movement of the early 1980s. In spite of the abstract language of deterrence, people came to see the absurdity of civil defense with shovels for what it was.

Nevertheless—in spite of public protest, *glasnost*, and *perestroika*, in spite of the freeze movement—enormous expenditure on arms continues, and the potential for mass destruction with an overabundance of nuclear warheads remains. A sober reminder of this fact is the U.S. government's (and the contractor's) conviction that, for the sake of national security, the Stealth bomber program (at $500 million per plane) must be saved, though this plane has never been flown and even though its partner, the B-1 bomber, is so flawed it had to be grounded—this in a time of federal budget "austerity" and an enormous federal deficit.

How do we explain such disproportionate defense expenditure in the context of improved superpower relations and growing evidence of domestic program neglect, such as a "war on drugs" with little money to support it? The concept of deterrence is central here. Deterrence policy presumes that the other side is not to be trusted, regardless of appearances (Gralnick 1988: 176–77). It says that progress in East–West relations has occurred primarily because of bargaining from a position of strength. In other words, nuclear arms assure peace by deterring the untrusted side from a first strike that would call for a return strike, culminating in nuclear holocaust. Millions upon millions of people seem to have accepted nuclear stockpiling as a necessary ingredient of deterrence policy, in spite of the obvious overkill capacity.

But with the emergence of the Gorbachev factor in the super-power equation, and with the rapid changes in Europe signaling the end of the Cold War, one can almost hear the world—as Gorbachev noted in his address to the United Nations—"breathe a sigh of relief." But even as the Iron Curtain falls and one after another Eastern European border opens, Frank Gaffney, director of the Center for Security Policy, asserts that the current Soviet missile deployment raises "serious questions about the viability of the American deterrent" and that the "much ballyhooed withdrawals of Soviet forces from Eastern Europe are not all they are cracked up to be" (1989). Nevertheless, since the real capability of nuclear holocaust is still very much with us, we can only hope that the current relief in world anxiety about superpower tension is more than just a pause.

There seems to be a complex interaction of several factors in operation here. People need and long for both personal and national security. Nuclear deterrence strategy is very abstract, and leaders assure citizens that the issue is too complex and important for their everyday concern. In such a context, omnicidal behavior patterns of denial and apathy come to dominate the majority's response in spite of a subliminal awareness that the world sits under the sword of Damocles, awaiting nuclear destruction (Solo 1988). With nuclear anxiety being aggravated by people's growing insecurity about threats to the environment and other crises such as the drug war and street violence, it is understandable why they would like to believe that the threat of global destruction is eliminated by the end of the Cold War initiated by Gorbachev.

But the truth is that the capability of nuclear destruction remains essentially the same today, in spite of an apparent respite in nuclear proliferation and superpower tensions. This is not to underestimate the enormous importance of Gorbachev's move to reduce Soviet military forces in Eastern Europe and on the Chinese border. His initiative provides a window of opportunity for dismantling military confrontation and nuclear superiority as a response to vulnerability and conflict. The relief felt worldwide after Gorbachev's decision that peace through strength (especially nuclear power) does not, in fact, leave individuals and the world more peaceful and secure.[2]

Creating a future without nuclear threat demands a strategy of prevention that goes beyond deterrence. Proponents of Star Wars, after all, argue that extending the nuclear arms race into space is worth the cost because it will prevent a first strike. Star Wars opponents—scientists, Physicians for Social Responsibility, and others—however, are equally convinced that the only safe and reasonable strategy is primary prevention as understood in public health terms (Hoff 1989: 23–25); that is, nuclear holocaust precludes the possibility of treatment or a return to community health. Therefore, the only sensible strategy is prevention (Adams and Cullen 1981).

The success of primary prevention implies distinguishing between natural disasters and those of human origin. Although individuals, families and whole communities can be devastated by natural disasters, survivors of tragedies such as the San Francisco earthquake are generally able to rise up from the rubble and to rebuild their lives and their communities. A key factor facilitating such coping with a natural disaster is the perception that the disaster is beyond anyone's control (Lifton and Olson 1976; Antonovsky 1980). Ordinarily it is interpreted as fate, bad luck, or an act of God. In other words, it is unpreventable and therefore one must simply move on (even though technology and economic resources can often mitigate the impact of natural disasters—Wijkman and Timberlake 1984). In striking contrast, disasters of human origin are preventable: what we have constructed we can dismantle. It is easy to lose sight of this fact after years of indoctrination about the necessity of nuclear deterrence policy. Our response pattern to this indoctrination for the past several decades has been that of passivity as dramatized in our Prologue scenario and in our studies revealing omnicidal personality patterns. But securing a future without nuclear threat entails our acknowledging the limits of deterrence and embracing prevention as the only viable strategy.

PROMOTING COMMON SECURITY

The beginnings of a change are already evident, particularly through the window of opportunity that the Gorbachev factor has provided in finding alternatives to the military approach to national security. Reexamining the familiar term "national security" can give us a clue to such an alternative, and introduce the notion of "Common Security." The era in which shovels for civil defense might have been taken seriously is over. The credibility of the superhawks has seriously eroded in the public view. A 1989 poll taken by the Survey Research Center of the University of Massachusetts revealed that 49 percent of those surveyed thought the government was spending too much on defense, and only 4.7 percent said too little. In contrast—despite a purported anti-tax attitude—83.1 percent of the respondents said they would support higher taxes for education; 71.9 percent would pay for expanded medical research; and 68 percent said they would pay more to hunt down drug dealers. On the other hand, 77.8 percent said no to more taxes to reduce the federal deficit (created primarily through the Reagan defense buildup).

These survey results suggest a definite shift away from public willingness to support a government that continues to spend 60 percent of its budget on defense.[3] It may be that the Gorbachev factor has led people to a false sense of lessened nuclear terror, simply out of relief that superpower tensions have eased. Nevertheless, such survey responses point to a grass-roots mentality that complements the new "beyond the Cold War" paradigm of Common Security (Solo 1988)—a paradigm that may hold important clues to a future without nuclear threat, and appears to address the need for coalition-building among peace activists.

Common Security as a formulation for change follows the path-breaking work of the Palme Commission (named after Olof Palme, the Prime Minister of Sweden, who has since been assassinated, purportedly because of his peace initiatives) and of diverse groups and individuals promoting peace. It presents a series of principles to guide thinking and action about peace beyond the

1980s. These principles imply a need to return to the original ethical standards of the United States when debating the role of its interests around the world.[4] They demand public debate on the fact that the United States currently has defense commitments to 118 countries, creating a U.S. role as "world policeman" and increasing the danger of nuclear response each time our national interests are threatened and need to be defended. The Common Security perspective raises the question of how these defense commitments relate to the insecurities of people in their everyday lives: drug terror, hazardous waste, the greenhouse effect and global warming.

Pam Solo (1988), chief spokesperson of Common Security principles, acknowledges their potential contradictions—for example, the simultaneous demand that nations be permitted self-determination and autonomy along with a call for stricter international standards of political, social, and economic rights. The principles also promote an anti-military bias while affirming a nation's right to self-defense. The point, though, is not to promote uniformity of thinking or to substitute the dominant militaristic confrontational mentality with a straightjacket of another sort. Rather, the principles are proposed as a guide away from the either/or (for example, Iron Curtain/Free World) mentality that has brought us to the brink of nuclear catastrophe.

Some of these principles are already contained in the U.N. charter. But they are less fruitful in promoting peace than they might be, because nationalistic interests often outweigh global issues and stymie any chance for united action to assure the common good. With common security versus national security as our key, however, the principles can help orchestrate a new national debate and citizen peace initiatives. Such a new paradigm can replace the "defense specialists know best" mentality that has nurtured omnicidal personality patterns of passivity and denial of nuclear peril. Common Security gives us an index for measuring violence-inducing behaviors (and the structural violence of poverty and oppression) and world peace–inducing behaviors. And it implies a series of steps to get from the freeze to a nonnuclear future. Such steps will inevitably be devised once a new way of thinking takes hold, and they will be tailored to the needs and political context of local grass-roots groups. A reorientation of family relationships and the development of peace studies programs in the schools, are central in promoting new visions of peace and strategies of nonviolence.

9

Scenarios and Strategies for Peace

VISIONS OF PEACE

In 1985 the *Christian Science Monitor* sponsored a peace essay contest, asking its readers to imagine that peace has come to the world by the year 2010 (Foell and Nenneman 1986). After making that leap into the future, the contestants were to look back over the intervening 25 years and come up with a cohesive description of how this peaceful world has been brought about.

Essays were judged primarily on the feasibility of the ideas. Thus, the participants were expected to be knowledgeable of the framework of international relations in the world today. This ruled out the creation of fairy tales and the use of deus ex machina with its performance of miracles.

The 1,300 people who participated in the contest shared one common belief: a peaceful world is attainable. Their peace scenarios can be analyzed along two dimensions:

1. The agency responsible for initiating peace:

    - Government or intergovernmental organization, such as the United Nations; or

    - Individuals—that is, grass-roots movements.

2. Specific events that led to peace:

    - A major disaster; or

• Cooperation between two or more nation-states.

There is always some overlap when it comes to the agency responsible for peace: all governmental actions are initiated by individuals—either directly from people within the government, or indirectly by people outside who are exerting their influence on the government. But contestants also envision changes brought about by individuals not just through trying to influence governments, but through a change of consciousness within the individual—and ultimately within enough individuals (the critical mass) to bring about changes in perception and action in personal, interpersonal, and international relations. This must be that new mode of thinking without which—as Einstein warned us—humankind will perish.

The events described as leading to peace fall into two broad categories: a highly pessimistic one and a more hopeful one. The majority see peace obtainable only through a disaster. It is sadly obvious that Hiroshima has not been taken as our text (Lifton and Falk 1982), since the threat of nuclear annihilation is still hanging above us. One may wonder why so many of the contestants think that a disaster today would have a greater effect than the lesson we should have learned from Hiroshima and Nagasaki. Did it happen too long ago and too far away? Have there been too many intervening years between the time when atomic bombs could devastate only designated areas and this time when our nuclear forces can scorch the Earth? Do we need to sacrifice millions of people every so often to remind us what a major disaster is like?

Let us hope that a nuclear exchange between India and Pakistan like that described by one of the contestants—Colorado Governor Richard Lamm—will not be necessary. As Lamm tells it, there were then few people left from the 20 or so nuclear detonations to carry the message, but the whole world witnessed the devastation via U.S. and Soviet satellites.

In those moments—with a horrified world glued to its television sets in homes or in windows of stores with TV sets—

came the horror of modern weapons. A myriad of people struck blind whose only mistake had been to look at the fireball. Into every world capital, country, town, village, barrio, ghetto, fravello, and most huts, the universality of suffering was dramatically played out before shocked eyes. Nuclear war, like Medusa, consumed all who looked it in the face. (Foell and Nenneman 1986: p. 23)

In Lamm's scenario, peace was not negotiated. It simply "burst on a stunned mankind. Multiple messiahs preached the common theme of peace on earth." He concludes that

peace is neither the absence of war nor the presence of a disarmament agreement. Peace is a change of heart. Both the Soviet Union and the United States simply stopped building new weapons and missiles. These were not weapons but suicide devices. (p. 25)

The salvation-through-disaster scenarios (the typical avoidance-approach model) do not revolve solely around cataclysmic nuclear events. Other peace catalysts are seen as environmental or economic catastrophes. The peace-through-cooperation scenarios focus primarily on superpower relations, involving cooperation through arms control agreements, cultural and scientific exchanges, trade agreements, joint space missions, and Third World projects—much along the lines of the principles of Common Security discussed in Chapter 8. In some scenarios, non-superpowers such as China, the Middle East, the two Germanies, or a united Europe become the agents of peace.

The most idealistic of the peace essays describe an enlightened, ethical sense of humanity that has been brought about by a change in consciousness—a new vision. This has effected a shift in perspective; the problems confronting us must be seen in a new light. World citizens who hold a conviction of personal responsibility for the well-being of the global community have emerged as a new center of power. After decades of believing through government persuasion that confrontation was necessary to preserve the American way of life and promote national interests, the public finally saw that the price was too high and the risk to planet Earth too great to continue the arms race. As Geoffrey Grimes, another contestant, puts it,

> Thinking globally, acting locally, and perceiving newly—the principles of a new internationalism—became a paradigm for key individuals throughout the world who . . . have accepted personal responsibility for world peace. Probably no other factor has been more important in neutralizing the dilemmas of stalemated national governments . . . than has been this new consciousness-lifting worldwide. (p. 149)

One of the most intriguing proposals—intriguing because of its simplicity and plausibility of execution—envisions citizen exchanges occurring between the United States and the Soviet Union. We could have a yearly exchange of 1 million students—the entire college sophomore class of the United States, say, for that of the Soviet Union, with the children of high-ranking government officials being included. Aside from the obvious hostage value of such an exchange, we would learn to know each other as people and often even as friends, rather than as unfamiliar strangers we so easily distrust. As essayist Jerome Pressman says in an appeal to the president, "Let's stop focusing only on weapons; let's talk 'sophomores.' The sophomores would love their Russian year abroad. The Russians might be intrigued with such a proposal" (p. 213).

As in the case of personal conflict, trust assumes the key role here in both preventing and resolving conflict, while trust rests on our knowledge of the other and our shared interests. Thus, from the sophomores' lived experience with Soviet citizens, they would learn to know them as people like ourselves who eat, sleep, make love, give birth, work all their lives, and bury their dead—rather than merely as the enemy bent on destroying us and the planet.

A more ambitious proposal would involve the exchange be-tween high-ranking U.S. and Soviet defense officials, to be placed on the highest levels of the opposing country's military structure. This would have the effect of a foolproof verification of any disarmament agreement, calm international military crises, and check any possible military intervention in the affairs of another country. The success of such a strategy has long been advocated by game theory, which shows that cooperation is ultimately more advantageous for all parties concerned than is competition.

Together, the essayists in the *Christian Science Monitor*'s con-test dramatically illustrate that peace-making and the building of alternative security systems cannot be left to government alone. They also reveal the creative power that may lie dormant in many of us and could incite new ideas to replace the either/or thinking that has dominated the past few decades.

As catalysts, these scenarios represent a first step in replacing nuclear terror with peace. But imagination is not enough. How do we translate these idealistic models of a world without nuclear threat into the fabric of our everyday lives? What is the dynamic process whereby large numbers of people may actually change their way of thinking? On a hopeful note, since the essay contest, some of the possible action plans that the essayists envisioned are currently being implemented. For example, thanks to the Gorbachev initiatives, the iron curtain has fallen, and world com-merce, travel, and cultural exchange are accelerating, signifying positive changes even before those envisioned by the essayists.

Pam Solo (1988) in her book on Common Security proposes four levels of movement beyond the nuclear freeze of the 1980s to a nuclear-free world in the twenty-first century:

1. expand public education about the risks and costs of the arms race;

2. promote a new public debate about the political role of the United States in a world concerned with common security, not just the protection of national interests;

3. promote policy options based on the new mode of common security;

4. promote international citizen initiatives such as those envisioned by the *Christian Science Monitor* essayists.

These strategies include measures to inform leaders of the national security system.

Among the superpowers especially, national security officials wield enormous influence in world affairs and are deeply invested in maintaining their power over policy decisions. Though not necessarily creative as leaders, these officials do take their cues from public opinion and are susceptible to public pressure when it is organized.[1]

In our search for a strategy that will actualize a nuclear-free world, we examine two fundamental domains of social life: the educational system, and the process of parenting. And we explore the pivotal role that these institutions have in teaching about nuclear threat and its relationship to other critical issues such as:

- environmental threat from pollution, nuclear power waste, and deforestation;
- the interdependence of national economies, poverty, and world hunger;
- despair, violence, and drug abuse; and
- the culture of violence, both personal and political.

These issues span the personal, interpersonal, and global realms. They are complexly connected, but—as noted throughout this book—the common thread among them is life in the nuclear age and the tone of despair and destruction engendered by the threat of universal extinction. While diverse activities are needed to bring about peace, widespread education about the roots of conflict, as well as a change in the practice of parenting, hold the most promise for eliminating global threat.

PEACE STUDIES AND RELATED ISSUES

Our optimism is bolstered by the fact that an extraordinary phenomenon has occurred within the short time span of just the past few years: the establishment and growth of peace studies programs in high schools and universities across the United States and in Europe. There has been a groundswell of educational activity that portends a true swing of the pendulum toward teaching and learning a new way of thinking about global issues.

Given the militaristic climate that has dominated for several decades, one wonders how peace studies could have emerged and why the movement is gaining such great momentum on campuses. Perhaps the phenomenon can be explained partially by people's weariness with war and violence, and their yearning for personal and national peace. Another key to the success of these peace studies has been the effort made to avoid reproducing a competitive mode in the curriculum of study. Students are encouraged to be creative and perform in accordance with their own standards of excellence, rather than trying simply to outdo others. For example, teachers create a "green light" atmosphere—a type of brainstorming session in which everyone's ideas are encouraged and valued. Such a climate—regardless of the study topic—can capture the attention of students whose cynicism about a future world all too often spills over into general burnout and lack of motivation for learning. Similar principles guide the work of Educators for Social Responsibility, though the focus of this group is on nonviolent conflict-resolution tactics for high school and elementary students.

Central to all peace studies programs, however—regardless of local interests and adaptation to the politically possible—is the common goal of introducing students to the importance of organizing their thoughts about peace, conflict, and the interconnectedness of global issues.[2] Thus, rather than a rigid either/or approach, which carries with it a vulnerability to liberal/conservative labeling and to accusations that the students are being brainwashed, academics stress a "both/and" examination of issues—confident that

informed graduates trained to think critically may avoid the omnicidal behavior pattern in their role as citizens.

Educators do not need to agree on a single approach to peace
studies. Indeed, the success of peace studies depends on our being
careful not to politicize the topic. Most important is a systematic
plan to include nuclear threat in the curriculum for explicit critical
examination and contextual analysis of its relationship to other
issues. Concepts of nuclear deterrence and war and peace may be
made more meaningful to students when connected to the issues
and concerns of their everyday lives—for example, the competition for success encountered in class, career, and personal relationships. Students may feel hopeless and powerless, or anxious about
the urban violence all around them, but still not relate these
personal experiences to larger social issues. Peace studies are
central in unraveling the connection between the global threat, and
personal experiences such as violence, hopelessness, substance
abuse, and suicide. As Leslie Cagan notes with regard to new
directions for the disarmament movement,

> We will not pull diverse groupings of people together into
> *sustained* political activity around disarmament (be it a lim-
> ited notion of nuclear disarmament or a more comprehensive
> definition) unless they see how such an effort is directly tied
> to other pressing issues in their lives. (Cagan 1983: 107;
> emphasis in original)[3]

NUCLEAR THREAT, POVERTY, HUNGER, AND CYNICISM

The studies of children and their fears about nuclear threat
support Cagan's point: people's concerns about everyday survival
issues such as crime and the effects of poverty take priority and
drown out the immediacy of nuclear threat. Thus—peace studies
notwithstanding—it will be difficult, if not impossible, to engage
citizens in the political process toward global security if, for
example, they are compelled by community violence and poverty

to focus their daily lives and activities on physical and economic survival. Many citizens are divided along class and racial lines and their exposure to neighborhood crime and the drug war. These obvious divisions may all too easily obscure what affects us in common: armaments expenditure at the expense of domestic concerns, and the inevitable communitywide influence of problems like the drug war and environmental pollution.

Regardless of a community's social or economic position, public education is needed about the relationship between the billions spent on arms and the consequent neglect of domestic investment in such things as jobs, high-quality public schools, drug treatment centers, and appropriate resources for the war on drugs. For example, in a family that makes a decent livelihood, a teenager with a real chance at success in school and a crime-free subsistence would be less vulnerable to the "quick fix" approach to economic survival—as, say, by renting a room for drug dealing. Individuals who entertain realistic hopes for future economic survival and an opportunity to contribute to society are also less vulnerable to suicidal despair, as noted in Chapter 4. And while poverty and other injustices do not excuse personal violence, social inequities do breed an atmosphere of cynicism in which problems like the reckless bravado of youth gangs and random violence flourish.

In poor and developing countries, the connection between daily survival and nuclear threat is dramatized in the masses of people dying every day of hunger while leaders squander their meager resources on arms and civil strife. As in prosperous nations, most of these people do not see the connection between their daily misery—their everyday fears—and a world dominated by greed and a mind-set of competition and aggression as a solution to conflict.

All over the world, neighborhoods, towns, and other groups will enhance their sense of control over their own destiny and that of the globe once they have invested their communal energy into a diversion of spending away from defense and toward the recovery and maintenance of their community and improvement of their everyday existence—in terms of schools, jobs, health insurance, youth programs, police protection, environmental cleanup, and preservation of the planet for future generations. Such conscious-ness-raising can occur not only through formal education pro-grams, but also in public forums and traditional service organizations such as the Lions Clubs, Rotary International, and so forth.

Thus, while each individual has the potential to make an enor-mous difference in global affairs, the prospect of this happening is greatly enhanced in a society that does not neglect the ordinary needs of the people in favor of defense expenditures. Global security implies an awareness of the fact that political conflict is often ignited by protest against economic, racial, and other injus-tices. In short, while social and economic disparities continue, significant numbers of people will be lost to action on behalf of world peace.

POWER RELATIONSHIPS

The issue of creating a context for peace studies leads us to a consideration of power itself—personal and political. In the tradi-tion of Max Weber, the prevailing concept of power involves the assertion of one's will over another. Implied in this view of power is the use of force, if necessary. In the domestic sphere, this is observed in violence against mates, or in powerless children and weak elders. In the political sphere, force is exercised through the power of police and the criminal justice system used by the state to enforce society's rules and to protect citizens.

Jean Baker Miller (1976), Sara Ruddick (1989), and others suggest a new concept of power that involves *asserting oneself while simultaneously nurturing the other*, instead of dominating her or him. This model of power does not deny conflict, but emphasizes cooperation, team work, and joint problem-solving—rather than winning and losing, giving orders, controlling and exploiting others. It complements the notion of conflict resolution that protects the conflicted parties, in contrast to the competitive mentality that always requires a winner and loser. An emphasis on such cooperative models starting in early childhood might profoundly influence the would-be winners and losers in the current superpower struggle.

In a similar vein, John Mack (1989) distinguishes two uses of the word "power." One connotes vitality—the driving force that expresses our "loving connection with other beings and our conviction that we can have a positive impact upon the world around us." The other implies the traditional relationship of domination and control—of resources, nature, and other creatures—and "finds its most extreme expression in the use of nuclear weapons as instruments of psychological terror" (Mack 1989: 1). If one's need for personal power and self-mastery is frustrated, then helplessness (a feature of the omnicidal personality pattern) is the inevitable result. For the most part, our sense of personal power and self-esteem develops through secure relationships within the family—which serve as prototypes for our later attachments to communities and the nation. The "patriotism" of people like T.K. Jones and members of the Committee on the Present Danger can be seen as an extreme expression of attachment to nation gone awry.[4] As Mack notes, the violent revolutions of threatened peoples attest to "the supreme power of ethno-national identifications" (p. 10).[5] While we do not know the personal life histories of those public persons who continue to support military confrontation as a protection of our national interests, we do know from the study of interpersonal violence that deep-seated personal insecurity figures in many aggressive acts, and collectively seems to contribute to a societywide climate of violence and aggression—as expressed, for example, in child abuse (Gil 1987, Rubenstein 1982). We also know that violence is much more probable so long as confrontation is the preferred mode of resolving conflict.

When intimate and family relationships breed violence and abuse instead of a sense of personal security, the personal and societal costs are high. A common theme expressed by victims of violence is that power was wielded over them—that they were ultimately rendered powerless. Emotional healing from abuse, therefore, must include regaining one's sense of personal power and mastery. It also requires that the victim come to interpret or make sense of the violence within her or his meaning structure—a process aided by public recognition that the abuse was unjustified and that the victim is entitled to compensation (Lifton 1967, Lifton and Olson 1976, Hoff 1990a, Sales, Baum, and Shore 1984). Failure to provide this recognition can contribute to emotional scarring and possibly more violence (the disempowering of others) as compensation for one's personal sense of violation and power-lessness. Carried into the political arena, the personal deficits and learned violence stemming from abuse complement the socially approved violence of military confrontation.

PARENTING PRACTICE

As suggested in Chapter 1, male/female differences in aggression can be traced to child-rearing patterns in which mothers play a primary role (Chodorow 1978, Keller 1983b). As a consequence of mother's dominant role in parenting, boys go through very different experiences than girls during the early stage of acquiring a sense of ego identity separate from that of mother. At this stage, boys learn that becoming a man is *not* being a woman (not being like mother); while for a girl, *who* she is depends much more directly on her intimate relationship with mother. Of particular relevance to the issue of aggression is that boys may experience their discontinuity from mother as violent. During the process of separating from mother, boys acquire a sense of the social deval-uation of motherhood, since "becoming me" requires not being like mother. Boys also learn the value of distance in human interaction—which may lay the foundation for adult difficulties in male–female intimacy. In human relations, this is often observed in men's overinvestment in the objective and rational world, in contrast to women's overinvestment in relationships—the emo-tional and personal (Flax 1983, Elshtain 1981).

In a related vein, Sara Ruddick (1983) postulates a relationship between "maternal practice" and modes of conflict resolution. In this argument, women are not naturally less violent than men.

Rather, as the primary caretakers of children, women—whether mothers or not—learn to mediate conflict between children with a primary goal of not only ending the fight, but of "conserving" (that is, protecting from destruction) both parties to the conflict. This mode of conflict resolution is diametrically opposite to the dominant competitive mode in which there is always a winner and a loser. The child caretaker's aim is to prevent the injury of either child. Ruddick links this repertoire of maternal practice in conflict mediation to the political arena. She argues that men's relative inexperience with child care and its conserving approach to conflict, along with the deliberate fostering of competitive values for boys and men and the relative absence of women in leadership positions, leaves the political realm of human relations singularly devoid of the benefits of maternal practice, and conversely oversupplied with competitive elements (see also LaFarge 1987).

This view of aggression also addresses the issue of female aggressive behavior in power positions—from wars declared by women heads of state, to the violence of some mothers against their children. That is, all human beings—male and female—are equally capable of aggression and violence, but child-rearing patterns suggest why "militant enthusiasm" is more often observed in men than in women (Reardon 1985).

Power relationships have, of course, a bearing on parenting practice. While the line between physical discipline and abuse is sometimes not very clear, it is clear that children who experience physical discipline—even from a loving parent—receive an early message that physical force is an acceptable solution to problem-solving and conflict resolution. The pervasiveness and persistence of this early message is highlighted by the fact that 90 percent of U.S. adults consider it impossible to rear a child without some physical discipline, despite extensive research pointing to its adverse effects. One cannot help but wonder just how much of this discipline is meted out in the belief that it is "for the good of the child," and how much to satisfy an adult's power needs.

In addition, many children observe the abuse of power and the exercise of physical violence between their parents, and are often victims of outright abuse themselves—a pattern exacerbated by alcohol and other drugs. Although all abused children do not become abusive themselves, most violent adults have a history of having been abused as children. In addition, violent conflict resolution learned in the family is bolstered by widespread violence in the media and society as a whole, including the ultimate violence of nuclear destruction that we have been led to believe may be "necessary" for national security. Thus—in a vicious cycle—the experience or observation of violence in the family creates, on the one hand, a context for socially approved aggression. On the other hand, socially approved violence such as war and capital punishment lends an aura of greater acceptability to violence at the personal and family level.

Nevertheless, what is learned can be unlearned and replaced with nonviolent tactics of conflict resolution. The family is the primary source of learning—whether about power, violence, or nonviolence under stress. A critical examination of power relationships in personal and societal contexts, then, is not only a key feature of peace and conflict studies, but is also central to the life skills that students will need as future parents. And in public universities especially, it is not uncommon to find students who are already parents and are struggling to escape disturbed family relationships through the route of higher education. So an essential complement to peace studies—if not an integral component— should be how to create and maintain peace in one's personal and family life.[6]

It would seem that, to find new ways of thinking about power, we must start with changes in our everyday personal relationships, and reach the point where every act of physical coercion is viewed as a criminal act—as is the case in Sweden with regard to the physical discipline of children. Peace studies curricula can have a pivotal impact on developing nonviolent strategies for managing stress and crises in ordinary social life. As a matter of fact, some changes in family structure have occurred during the past few decades—at least in some social strata—away from an absolute hierarchy to a more egalitarian structure. As Ruddick (1989) and

others envision, when egalitarian parenting becomes common-
place rather than exceptional, when parents share both the burden
and the power of parenting, when both parents have routine
opportunities to mediate children's conflict while also nurturing
them, when children learn to assert themselves without hurting the
other, then there will be a greater chance of extending nonviolent
conflict resolution to the political arena in strategies for global
security (Solo 1988). But the change in traditional power relationships comes slowly.

The traditional view of power as control over others is seductive
not only for those who control, but also for the controlled—which
suggests one of the reasons why people resist change. Those who
control others do not usually do so, at least in modern society,
without a certain acquiescence from the oppressed. To the extent
that people are unconscious of their acquiescence, their response
can be seen as "oppressed group behavior" (Freire 1970, 1973)—a
phenomenon in which people come to believe and act on what
those in power say about them and their role in society (for
example: nuclear issues are too complex for the everyday person;
those in government know best). Paulo Freire's concept of oppressed group behavior supports our findings about omnicidal
personality patterns and the tendency toward passivity and acceptance of leaders' views.

For some, the need to be directed by others is linked to personal
insecurity and fear, and the need to avoid responsibility. For many,
however, it is simply easier to let those in charge continue to run
things, as they themselves get on with the task of everyday survival. But this is precisely where the greatest danger lies in regard
to the nuclear threat. Leaving the issue to those who claim superior
knowledge about global politics—not to mention military
power—may be consistent with a pattern of inaction and passivity
regarding controversial issues in general: it is too much trouble, or
too threatening, or simply too overwhelming to face. In the case
of nuclear threat, the odds of total annihilation through these
omnicidal tendencies are just too high to allow us to remain in
hiding under a false security blanket.

REPLACING AGGRESSION WITH COOPERATION

But the mere absence of physical violence in childhood and family relationships is not sufficient to sensitize children to global concerns. Also needed are a parental consciousness of peace issues and a deliberate attempt to parent in such a way that children grow up responsive to social issues including nuclear threat, environmental hazards, sex-role stereotypes, race relations, and so on.

In Chapter 4 we cited the interviews of LaFarge (1987) with parents and children regarding nuclear anxieties, and how parents must break away from pretending to themselves that not talking about the nuclear threat will somehow lessen their children's fears. But consciousness-raising about nuclear issues does not exist in a family or sociocultural vacuum. According to Kathy and Jim McGinnis (1981), peace issues are one part of a parenting pattern that is complex and fraught with frustration at many levels since there is so little support for it beyond the family itself. As Kathy McGinnis writes,

> The children and I were driving to a shopping center. On the way we passed the offices and plant of an aircraft manufacturer in our area, whose main business was in military contracts. The children asked what kind of work people did there. In answering their questions, I included my opinion about the defense industry. I said I wished a company like this would use more of its resources making commercial airplanes and other peace-related items. I said I wished they did not make bombers and fighter planes. (McGinnis and McGinnis 1981: 41)

Kathy McGinnis's children responded: "We have to have bombs! We have to be able to get the enemy so they can't get us. Bombs will help us fight!" (p. 41)

Clearly these children had absorbed the prevailing "us against them" mentality of the larger society despite their parents' conscious efforts to instill the opposite values through such tactics as avoiding physical discipline and war toys, monitoring and discussing television violence, sensitizing the children to an international perspective with the aid of devices like a home globe, and staging family celebrations around such occasions as U.N. Day. So pervasive is the confrontational approach that, in spite of deliberate attention to peace issues in their parenting, the McGinnises discovered that one of their children had written a letter to President Carter asking him to

> please send the Shah back to Iran. . . . I don't want 50 people killed from our country because the shah is one person and the Iraniumas [sic] will kill the shah if we send him over. But if we don't send him over they'll kill 50 Americans and 50 is more than one so if they kill one person it will save 50 people. (McGinnis and McGinnis 1981: 51)

Central to "parenting for peace and justice" is the conviction that competitive behavior need no longer continue as the norm, once the myth of the aggressive instinct has been abandoned. Still, teaching children to think in terms of cooperation is sometimes like swimming upstream (McGinnis and McGinnis 1981, Judson 1984).

Nevertheless, the family is the place to begin preparing potential members of the critical mass necessary to institute real change. The peace-building process must be based on a real awareness of the connection between personal, family, and global issues. Peace studies and egalitarian family relations complement each other in making these connections visible. In general, people in the United States are fed up with street crime, drugs, inadequate school systems, homelessness, and a health care system in crisis. But it is unlikely that much impact will be made on these domestic issues so long as most government dollars are siphoned off for an insecure defense system. To the extent that people see connections between the concrete concerns of their everyday lives and global security issues, to that extent will they be less likely to continue in the omnicidal patterns that threaten our future.

Appendix

Table A.1
Nuclear Attitude Scale Analysis of Differences between the Before and After Conditions in the Correlated Sample

N	Sex	Age	Before Condition Score	Before Condition Mean	After Condition Score	After Condition Mean	
48	F	16-30	+435	+9	+684	+14	(a)
27	F	32-64	+278	+10	+446	+16	(b)
29	M	18-30	+172	+6	+281	+10	(c)
20	M	31-62	+6	+0.3	+6	+0.3	

(a) $\propto$ >.001; A = .0899 df 47.
(b) $\propto$ >.01; A = .166 df 26.
(c) $\propto$ >.01; A = .119 df 28.

Increase in scores (or means) reflect increases in anti-nuclear attitudes.

Table A.2
Nuclear Attitude Scale Analysis of Differences between the Before and After Conditions of Two Independent Samples

	N	Sex	Age	Before Condition Score	Mean	N	Sex	Age	After Condition Score	Mean
	43	F	15-30	474	+11	24	F	18-29	273	+11
	29	F	31-59	338	+11.6	25	F	30-55	357	+14
	29	M	15-29	134	+ 4.6	24	M	18-29	175	+7
	34	M	31-66	30	+ 0.8	25	M	31-65	243	+9.7
Total	135		15-66	976	+ 7.2	98		18-65	1,048	10.8*

*$\propto$ >.01; t = 2.488 df 230

Means reflect the relative amount of anti-nuclear attitudes.

Table A.3
Rank Order of Anti-nuclear Scores on the Ten Nuclear Attitude Items under Before and After Conditions in Correlated and Independent* Populations**

Items	Rank Before		After		Rank Changes	
1. Nuclear annihilation is an abstract concept . . . (disagree)	1	(2)	1	(2)	0	(0)
2. As long as we have nuclear missiles in Europe . . . . . (disagree)	9	(10)	5	(7)	+4	(+3)
3. If the only choice is between unilateral disarmament . . . (agree)	2	(1)	2.5	(1)	-.5	(0)
4. Any consequence is better than destruction . . . . (agree)	5	(5)	9	(6)	-4	(-1)
5. The survival of future generations is more important . . . . .(agree)	7.5	(8)	8	(8)	-.5	(0)
6. If there is a nuclear confrontation, I would feel relieved . . . . (agree)	4	(6)	10	(9)	- 6	(-3)
7. All we need is first strike capacity . . . .(disagree)	3	(3)	2.5	(3)	+.5	(0)
8. We must be willing to run the risk . . . .(disagree)	10	(9)	7	(10)	+3	(-1)
9. The real enemy today is not communism . . . .(agree)	6	(7)	6	(4)	0	(+3)
10. We have no right to carry the struggle . . . .(agree)	7.5	(4)	4	(5)	+3.5	(-1)

*Independent population rankings are the numbers in parentheses.
**Plus (+) signs reflect the increase in anti-nuclear scores on a given scale, while minus (-) signs reflect a decrease in anti-nuclear score (or an increase in pro-nuclear score) on that scale, after viewing "The Day After.

Disagreement with items 1, 2, 7, and 8 and agreement with items 3, 4, 5, 6, 9, and 10 received plus (+) scores and are taken to infer an anti-nuclear attitude; while agreement with items 1, 2, 7, and 8 and disagreement with items 3, 4, 5, 6, 9, and 10 received minus (-) scores, inferring a pro-nuclear attitude.

Table A.4
Responses to the Nuclear War Questionnaire: Some Highlights of
Responses Derived from 461 Questionnaires before and after Viewing
"The Day After" (in percent)

	BEFORE	AFTER
1. Probability of N.W.* in your life		
Inevitable/Impossible (0% chance)	12	5
Likely/Possible	84	92
2. Frequency of thinking about N.A. **		
Daily/Often	10	28
Hardly Ever	44	29
Sometimes	34	42
3. Consequences of NW.		
Limited Damage	20	12
Extinguish life &/or planet	59	70
4. Survival preference		
Survive under all conditions	13	9
" w/o physical suffering	35	35
Die at impact	31	34
Die before impact	17	22
7. Nuclear weapons in your area make you feel		
More safe	26	21
Less safe	68	71
8. Casualty acceptance to retaliate attack on ally		
100% of your population killed	7	9
50 - 75% killed	3	3
10 - 25% "	6	9
Up to 1% killed	14	19
Any casualties unacceptable	70	60
9. Energy investment to prevent N.W.		
None	43	38
Some	33	41
Extreme	21	21
10. Death by N.A. more tragic than personal death		
No	28	24
Yes	72	76

* N.W. (Nuclear War)
** N.A. (Nuclear Annihilation)

Percentages do not always add up to 100: not all choices are presented here; also responses were omitted or are uninterpretable.

Table A.5
Distribution of Suicide/Omnicide Survey Sample Population

	Suicide	Omnicidal	Survivor	Omni/Suicide	TOTAL
Mean Age	29	31	31	27	
N	38	101	77	26	242
Percentage	15	42	32	11	100

Table A.6
Frequency of Responses to Critical Items on the Suicide/Omnicide Questionnaire (in percent)

	Suicidal		Omnicidal		Survivor		Combined Suic/Omni	
1. Thinking about own death**								
Daily/weekly	34	(13)	21	(21)	20	(15)	54	(14)
Hardly ever	23	(9)	43	(43)	43	(39)	15	(4)
2. Thinking about nuclear annihil.***								
Daily/weekly	37	(14)	11	(11)	5	(4)	31	(8)
Hardly ever	34	(13)	65	(65)	44	(33)	46	(13)
3. Nuclear war in one's lifetime probability*								
High	23	(9)	11	(11)	18	(14)	38	(10)
Low	29	(11)	53	(54)	43	(33)	27	(7)
4. Energy investment								
Low (none)	5	(1)	36	(36)	12	(9)	54	(14)
High	50	(19)	20	(20)	38	(29)	15	(4)
5. Worst about nuclear war*								
Unnecessary	55	(21)	44	(45)	75	(58)	42	(11)
Powerlessness	10	(4)	29	(29)	12	(9)	8	(2)
6. Greatest tragedy								
Beloved's death	44	(17)	62	(63)	44	(34)	58	(15)
Nuclear annihilation	50	(19)	28	(28)	41	(32)	31	(8)

*∝ >.05; **∝>.01; ***∝>.001

1. Statistical comparisons refer only to suicidal and omnicidal categories of target items.

2. Numbers in parentheses refer to actual number of respondents.

3. Percentages do not add up to 100 since semi-openended questions allowed for some idiosyncratic responses.

Notes

CHAPTER 1

1. See R. J. Lifton's discussion of "Anger, Rage, and Violence" in *The Broken Connection* (1979: ch. 12, p. 156).

2. The urge in all that is animate to return to its former, inanimate state is a Freudian fallacy. There is no return. Once an organism has been formed and has lived, its death does not reinstate the never-having-lived condition.

3. Some communal living institutions may represent an exception. Also, it is becoming increasingly common in management circles to emphasize collaborative, rather than dominant, hierarchical relationships between employers and employees.

4. J. K. Galbraith (1981) has argued that the arms race has deeply damaging effects on the U.S. free enterprise system: arms production has not strengthened the economy, but rather greatly weakened it. Military expenditures have been drawing resources at a cost to domestic uses—starving industrial plants of capital, for example, and thus weakening the country's competitive edge as well as world prestige.

This point also applies to the need for diversion of defense spending toward economic aid and debt relief to the countries currently insisting on greater political freedom and access to consumer goods. As Galbraith has said recently, "Vested pecuniary, political and intellectual interest will not yield easily to the new reality" (1989: 3).

CHAPTER 2

1. Adam and Eve "begat" only after they were thrown out of the Garden of Eden. God feared that, after having eaten from the Tree of Knowledge—and

thus knowing good and evil—they might also partake of the Tree of Life and live forever.

CHAPTER 3

1. John Somerville (1979, 1982) was apparently the first to use the term "omnicide." It is a manifestation of the zeitgeist that we the authors coined the term "omnicide" prior to our knowing of Somerville's work.

CHAPTER 4

1. See M. Deutsch's review of research (1985: 57–58); also J. Goldering and R. Doctor (1985: 119–21), Schwebel (1982), Mack and Beardslee (1982), and Chivian and Snow (1983).

CHAPTER 5

1. Phyllis LaFarge cites the appeal of fundamentalism when developments in the "big world" take on the appearance of prophecy: "The worst may happen to you, but you, the individual believer, will be saved" (1987: 80).

2. In Part III we discuss in more detail the credibility problem that any peace movement will have with mainstream Americans when it appears to be polarized into an "us and them" mentality. We then suggest strategies for dealing with the threat to our common security, regardless of ideology.

3. Rank order correlation coefficients between the two population samples are significant at the .01 level for the before condition (rho .87) as well as for the after condition (rho.81). Thus, with conditions held constant, the degree of pro- or anti-nuclear rating of each item is consistent across both sample populations. On the other hand, a rank order correlation assessing the relation between the two conditions (before and after) as rated by the *same* respondents showed no significant correlation, indicating a change in pro- or anti-nuclear score elicited by the particular scale item as a function of the after condition. The Sandler A-test was used for analyzing the correlated sample, and the t-test for the independent sample. (See Table A.3 in the Appendix.)

4. Percentages do not always add up to 100. Some responses cannot be interpreted, as in cases of more than one response or "other."

5. It is interesting to compare these responses with those given by children, as discussed in Chapter 4. As children grow older, they remember less and less about nuclear-related dreams—presumably repressing the topic in the same coping and survival tactic that many adults use.

CHAPTER 6

1. See the Prologue and Chapter 3.

2. Strictly speaking, the term "suicide attempt" should be limited to those who *intend* and attempt to commit suicide, but fail to do so for unforeseen reasons such as rescue. The term "parasuicide" is more accurate for those who injure themselves but do not intend to die.

3. The ratio of actual suicides to suicide attempts is roughly 1 or 2:10. Suicide statistics, however, are highly variable cross-culturally; and reported figures are generally regarded as underestimates because of continuing taboos, insurance bias, and so forth. See Hoff (1989: 175–78 and 203–04).

4. "Suicidal" as defined here refers to a much broader concept than the usual one of more or less imminent risk of self-destruction in response to acute emotional turmoil. It includes those who have a generally more accepting disposition toward suicide.

5. In terms of suicide—while it is a national public-health problem and probably undercounted—the *majority* of people in the total population are survivors. Conversely, in terms of omnicide—since there is still no widespread protest movement against the arms race and nuclearism—we infer that the *minority* of people in the general population are survivors.

6. Adding to this complex dynamic is the potential impact of the media and pop culture on young people and on the epidemic of youth suicide—a subject of continuing debate in suicidology circles. See Hoff (1990b).

CHAPTER 7

1. The fact that the same items were criticized equally often as biased to the left as to the right gave us an added assurance of working with a balanced instrument.

2. As a matter of fact, 17 attitude scales had to be discarded for the computation of attitude scores. In part, the German response to the instrument can be explained by the inherent limitations of forced-choice items on survey instruments. In contrast to more qualitative approaches to research, surveys provide much less access to the nuances and complex meanings that respondents may attach to particular items or topics.

3. Since previous observations indicated that attitudes toward nuclear war issues are influenced by current events—at least temporarily (as after the television show "The Day After")—we conducted an additional survey of 150 people in the United States within the same time frame as those conducted in Germany and in France (1987), for the sake of any comparisons we draw between countries. We also added the adapted question 8 as a new item on the U.S. survey.

4. This response may be influenced in part by cultural differences in esti-
mating the value of surveys versus more qualitative approaches, as discussed in
note 2 above in reference to the German response.

5. One may recall the French reaction of leniency toward their intelligence
operatives who sunk a Greenpeace ship (resulting in the death of a photographer)
to prevent any interference with their nuclear bomb tests off the New Zealand
coast. The perpetrators were sentenced to prison by a New Zealand court, but
the French government succeeded in having them transferred to France under
the condition that they would be kept in prison for the duration of their
sentence—only to set them free a short time after their arrival in France.

CHAPTER 8

1. Although the idea of fighting and winning a nuclear war is less and less
credible with the public, Robert Scheer's 1982 book about the shovel notion is
historically important as it reveals the continuity among administration and
congressional leaders regarding deterrence and thus the need for a "strong
defense."

Thomas K. Jones, deputy under secretary of defense for research and engi-
neering in the Reagan administration, was a spokesperson of the Committee on
the Present Danger—a group of "cold warriors," superhawks, who finally
gained an inside track of influence to the highest circles of U.S. government.
The committee put an aura of intellectual respectability on what otherwise might
have been perceived by the public as out-of-date 1950s style anti-communist
ravings. They also fueled Ronald Reagan's idea that the Soviet menace was a
simple elaboration of his experience of the communist influence on the screen-
actors guild in the 1950s. Many of the committee's members (for example,
Eugene Rostow) came from disillusionment with the radical socialist left. They
viewed the détente and disarmament of the 1970s as the most dangerous decade,
in contrast to the "good old days" of nuclear superiority right after the Cuban
missile crisis. They either missed or ignored the fact that nuclear superiority has
not necessarily meant more geopolitical influence. For instance, the Soviets had
been exerting quite a lot of influence over China, but they lost their place there
during the 1960s when their nuclear power increased.

T. K. Jones's assertion, "If there are enough shovels to go around,
everybody's going to make it" was based on the supposed Soviet civil defense
system and involved digging holes in the ground, covering them somehow with
a couple of doors, and throwing dirt on top to provide adequate fallout shelters
for the millions of Americans who would have to be evacuated from the cities
to the countryside (Scheer 1982: 18).

An adequate civil defense is thus key to those who argue that nuclear war is
survivable. This argument also obscures the difference between nuclear and

conventional war, and ignores the testimony of Physicians for Social Responsibility regarding the devastation of human and material resources to treat casualties, while naively suggesting instead that people can depend on their knowledge of first aid (pp. 111–13).

In any case, these hawks in the Reagan/Bush administration assumed a Soviet nuclear buildup in readiness for a first strike, but the facts are not all that clear. Much was inferred from U.S. intelligence data. The cold warriors of the Reagan/Bush team had an intellectual obsession with the "evil" of the Soviets, consonant with Reagan's labeling of the Soviet Union as the "evil empire." They equated the Soviets with Hitler, and asserted that nuclear war is winnable—despite all scientific evidence to the contrary. They saw the world in either/or terms—either the Iron Curtain or the Free World—reminiscent of the Stalinist era. A deep ethnocentrism pervaded their thinking: all evil resides within the communist enemy, and all virtue prevails at home. Their obsession with intellectual debates about the Soviets and deterrence led to their willingness to risk at least 20 million dead in the United States.

Scheer points out the contradiction between this perspective and the personal life-styles of Richard Pipes, T. K. Jones, and others in the Committee on the Present Danger. For example, (the Team B chairman of the Committee) Pipes was quoted as saying he is "much more worried about his children driving safely, and not getting sick, than nuclear war. He has never thought of building a bomb shelter" (p. 65). Scheer suggests it is possible that they "don't really believe their own alarmist rhetoric about the Soviet nuclear threat and the 'window of vulnerability.' " They seem to be "hostages to their own rhetoric" (p. 121). Scheer concludes that

> discussions of global violence come to seem absurdly—not to say hideously—abstract when these theorists discuss the prospect of mass destruction as something apart from actual metal tearing human flesh and bodies radiated to oblivion as millions upon millions die either in a blinding flash or unimaginable prolonged agony. (Scheer 1982: 120–21)

2. The sheer number of peace organizations (150 in the Greater Boston area alone) seems to symbolize the fundamental desire for peace among the masses, and reflects a healthy diversity and initiative to ward allaying anxiety about personal and national security.

3. Recently, the U.S. defense secretary proposed a small decrease in the defense budget, apparently in response to the dramatic political changes in Eastern Europe.

4. See Sissela Bok's *A Strategy for Peace* (1989), in which she appeals for renewed attention to the fundamental human values that have traditionally promoted the cohesion and survival of communities under stress.

CHAPTER 9

1. See Chapter 3 and also Chapter 8, note 1.

2. Academics' arrival at this common goal is all the more remarkable in the conservative climate that has dominated the 1980s campus and even gave rise to Accuracy in Academia, a watchdog group to keep tabs on too liberal professors. In such a climate, "peace studies" was easily discredited as a soft (read "not very important") subject in comparison to the hard sciences. Early in the movement, traditionalists interpreted peace studies to be a product of the liberal left–which sometimes evoked apology on the part of its advocates. Partly as a defense and partly as a reflection of real differences on how to address the issues, academics have argued about the name and focus of courses. Thus, programs have been titled variously peace studies (let's call it what it is and balance out the historic emphasis on war), peace and conflict studies (the study of peace implies the study of h‾ · to resolve conflict—destructive and nondestructive means), and peace and ɔcial justice studies (there can be no peace without social justice).

3. Illustrating this point, a number of peace studies faculty members have expressed their conviction that a prelude to students' engagement in peace and global issues is a peaceful personal existence in their university setting. That is, an environment must be created in which they feel valued and unthreatened by colleagues as well as by university personnel. In that vein—on urban campuses especially—programs are being developed to protect students from muggings and other attacks, along with peer counseling and other forms of assistance to victims of acquaintance rape (the wide incidence of which has recently come to public attention). Professors and counseling staff also note the toll taken on students by their unstable family situations, where battering and sexual abuse are all too common. Thus, removal of personally threatening situations is seen as a prerequisite to immersing oneself in world affairs.

4. See Chapter 8, note 1.

5. While the Iron Curtain has collapsed, we observe the potential for further violence to emerge from threats to the ethno-national identities that are rooted in historical rivalries between the European nation-states—rivalries often submerged in recent decades by the larger balance of terror between the superpowers.

6. This point is illustrated in the University of California peace curriculum in health sciences. Professor Warren Schonfeld stresses the intimate connection between peace and health at several levels. The first level is that of survival, as Physicians for Social Responsibility has illustrated. The second level focuses on health and social measures to achieve balance and harmony in contrast to the imbalance brought about by conflict and exploitation, as in family violence. The third level deals with a promotion of health that includes political action and the

three Ms: medication, meditation, and mediation. It seems clear that healing our planet includes healing and caring for ourselves.

References

Adams, R., and Cullen, S. eds. *The Final Epidemic: Physicians and Scientists on Nuclear War*. Chicago: Educational Foundation for Nuclear Science, 1981.

Antonovsky, A. *Health, Stress and Coping*. San Francisco: Jossey-Bass, 1980.

Bethe, H. A. "The technological imperative." *Bulletin of Atomic Scientists* 41: August 1985, 34–36.

Bok, S. *A Strategy for Peace: Human Values and the Threat of War*. New York: Pantheon, 1989.

Broverman, I. K., et al. "Sex-role stereotypes and clinical judgments of mental health." *Journal of Consulting and Clinical Psychology* 34: 1970, 1–7.

Cagan, L. "Feminism and militarism." In *Beyond Survival: New Directions for the Disarmament Movement*. M. Albert and D. Dellinger, eds. Boston: South End Press, 1983.

Charney, I. W. *How Can We Commit the Unthinkable—Genocide: The Human Cancer*. New York: Hearst Books, 1982.

Chivian, E., and Goodman, J. "What Soviet children are saying about nuclear war." IPPNW *Report* Winter 1984, 10–12. (International Physicians for the Prevention of Nuclear War, 225 Longwood Avenue, Boston, MA 02115.)

Chivian, E., and Snow, R. *There Is a Nuclear War Going On inside Me: What Children Are Saying about Nuclear Weapons*. Boston: International Physicians for the Prevention of Nuclear War, 1983.

Chodorow, N. *The Reproduction of Mothering: Psychoanalysis and the Sociology of Gender*. Berkeley: University of California Press, 1978.

Coles, R. "Children and the bomb." *New York Times Magazine*, December 8, 1985, 44–46, 54, 61–62.

Deutsch, M. "Some methodological considerations in studies of children and the threat of nuclear war." In *The Impact of the Threat of Nuclear War on Children and Adolescents.* Boston: International Physicians for the Prevention of Nuclear War, May 1985.

Dinnerstein, D. *The Mermaid and the Minotaur: Sexual Arrangements and Human Malaise.* New York: Harper Colophon Books, 1977.

Durkheim, E. *Suicide.* 2nd ed. New York: Free Press, 1951. (J. A. Spaulding and G. S. Simpson trans.; first published in 1897.)

Ehrenreich, B., and English, D. *For Her Own Good: 150 Years of the Experts' Advice to Women.* New York: Anchor Books, 1979.

Elshtain, J. B. *Public Man, Private Woman: Women in Social and Political Thought.* Princeton, NJ: Princeton University Press, 1981.

Escalona, S. "Children and the threat of nuclear war." In *Behavioral Science and Human Survival.* M. Schwebel, ed. Palo Alto, CA: Behavioral Science Press, 1965.

———. "Growing up with nuclear war." *American Journal of Orthopsychiatry* 52(4): 1982, 600–07.

Flax, J. "Political philosophy and the patriarchal unconscious: A psychoanalytic perspective on epistemology and metaphysics." In *Discovering Reality: Feminist Perspectives on Epistemology, Metaphysics, Methodology, and Philosophy of Science.* S. Harding and M. B. Hintikka, eds. Dordrecht, Holland/Boston: D. Reidel, 1983.

Foell, E., and Nenneman, R. *How Peace Came to the World.* Cambridge, MA: MIT Press, 1986.

Freire, P. *Education for Critical Consciousness.* Center for the Study of Development and Social Change, trans. New York: Continuum Press, 1973. (Original work published 1968.)

———. *Pedagogy of the Oppressed.* M. B. Ramon, trans. New York: Continuum Press, 1970. (Original work published 1968.)

Gaffney, F. J. "Is Moscow cutting its military? No, it's building up." *New York Times,* November 17, 1989, A39.

Galbraith, J. K. "Economics of the arms race—and after." In *The Final Epidemic.* R. Adams and S. Cullen, eds. Chicago: Educational Foundation for Nuclear Science, 1981.

———. "When capitalism meets communism, credos are shaken: Europe's changes force us to rethink beliefs." *Boston Sunday Globe,* December 3, 1989, A2.

Gerhardt, U. "Coping and social action: Theoretical reconstruction of the life-event approach." *Sociology of Health and Illness* 1: 1979, 195–225.

Gil, D. "Sociocultural aspects of domestic violence." In *Violence in the Home: Interdisciplinary Perspectives.* M. Lystad, ed. New York: Brunner/Mazel, 1987.

Goldering, J., and Doctor, R. "California adolescents' concerns about the threat of nuclear war." In *The Impact of the Threat of Nuclear War on*

Children and Adolescents. Boston: International Physicians for the Prevention of Nuclear War, 1985.

Goodman, L. M. "Attitudes towards nuclear war: Before and after 'The Day After.' " In *Symposium: Psychology and the Nuclear Threat*. 92nd Annual Convention of the American Psychological Association in Toronto, Canada, August 1984.

———. "Attitudes towards Suicide and Omnicide: A Comparison." 13th International Congress of Suicide Prevention and Crisis Intervention, Vienna, Austria, July 1985.

———. "Development of awareness of the nuclear threat in urban children." *Second Annual Conference on the Urban Mission: Problems and Perspectives*. Institute for Urban Research, Jersey City State College, Jersey City, NJ, April 1987, p. 60.

Goodman, P. *Growing Up Absurd*. New York: Random House, 1960.

Gralnick, A. "Trust, deterrence, realism, and nuclear omnicide." *Political Psychology* 9 (1): 1988, 175–88.

Hoff, L. A. *Battered Women as Survivors*. London: Routledge, 1990a.

———. "Crisis assessment and intervention for suicidal adolescents." In *Suicide Prevention in Schools*. A. Leenaars and S. Wenckstern, eds. Washington: Hemisphere Publishing, 1990b.

———. *People in Crisis*. 3rd ed. Redwood City, CA: Addison-Wesley, 1989.

Holmborg, P. O. and Bergstrom, A. "How Swedish teenagers think and feel concerning the nuclear threat." In *The Impact of the Threat of Nuclear War on Children and Adolescents*. Proceedings of an International Research Symposium, Helsinki-Espoo, 1984, pp. 170–80. (Copyright © International Physicians for the Prevention of Nuclear War, 1985.)

Hubbard, R. "Have only men evolved?" In *Discovering Reality: Feminist Perspectives on Epistemology, Metaphysics, Methodology, and Philosophy of Science*. S. Harding and M. B. Hintikka, eds. Dordrecht, Holland/Boston: D. Reidel, 1983.

Husserl, E. *Ideen zu einer reinen phaenomenologie*. The Hague: Martinus Nijhoff, 1950 (1913), vol. 1, p. 483.

Judson, S., ed. *A Manual on Nonviolence and Children*. Philadelphia: New Society Publishers, 1984.

Keller, E. F. *A Feeling for the Organism: The Life and Work of Barbara McClintock*. New York: Freeman, 1983a.

———. "Gender and science." In *Discovering Reality: Feminist Perspectives on Epistemology, Metaphysics, Methodology, and Philosophy of Science*. S. Harding and M. B. Hintikka, eds. Dordrecht, Holland/Boston: D. Reidel, 1983b.

———. *Reflections on Gender and Science*. New Haven/London: Yale University Press, 1985.

LaFarge, P. *The Strangelove Legacy: The Impact of the Nuclear Threat on Children*. New York: Harper and Row, 1987.

Lifton, R. J. *The Broken Connection: On Death and One Continuity of Life*. New York: Simon & Shuster, 1979.

———. *Death in Life*. New York: Random House, 1967.

Lifton, R. J., and Falk, R. *Indefensible Weapons: The Political and Psychological Case against Nuclearism*. New York: Basic Books, 1982.

Lifton, R. J., and Olson, E. "The human meaning of total disaster: The Buffalo Creek experience." *Psychiatry* 39: 1976, 1–18.

McGinnis, K., and McGinnis, J. *Parenting for Peace and Justice*. Maryknoll, NY: Orbis Books, 1981.

Mack, J. "Reflections on two kinds of power." Center for Psychological Studies in the Nuclear Age *Center Review* Winter 1989.

Mack, J., and Beardslee, W. R. *The Impact on Children and Adolescents of Nuclear Developments*. In Task Force Report No. 20. R. Rogers et al., eds. Washington, DC: American Psychiatric Association, 1982.

Miller, J. B. *Toward a New Psychology of Women*. Boston: Beacon Press, 1976.

Moss, N. *Men Who Play God: The Story of the H Bomb and How the World Came to Live with It*. New York: Harper and Row, 1968.

Okin, S. M. *Women in Western Political Thought*. Princeton, NJ: Princeton University Press, 1979.

Reardon, B. A. *Sexism and the War System*. New York/London: Teachers College Press, 1985.

Roberts, S. J. "Oppressed group behavior: Implications for nursing." *Advances in Nursing Science* 5 (7): 1983, 21–30.

Rubenstein, C. "Real men don't earn less than their wives." *Psychology Today* 16: 1982, 36–41.

Ruddick, S. *Maternal Thinking: Towards a Politics of Peace*. Boston: Beacon Press, 1989.

———. "Preservative love and military destruction: Some reflections on mothering and peace." In *Mothering: Essays in Feminist Theory*. J. Tribilcot, ed. Totowa, NJ: Rowman and Allenheld, 1983.

Sales, E., Baum, M., and Shore, B. "Victim adjustment following assault." *Journal of Social Issues*, 40 (1): 1984, 117–36.

Scheer, R. *With Enough Shovels: Reagan, Bush, and Nuclear War*. New York: Vintage Books, 1982.

Schwebel, M. "Nuclear cold war: Student opinions and professional responsibility." In *Behavioral Science and Human Survival*. M. Schwebel, ed. Palo Alto, CA: Behavioral Science Press, 1965.

Shneidman, E. *Definitions of Suicide*. New York: Wiley, 1985.

Small, C. *Mary Shelley's Frankenstein: Tracing the Myth*. Pittsburg: University of Pittsburg Press, 1973.

Snow, D. P. *The Necessary Peace: Nuclear Weapons and Superpower Relations.* Lexington, MA: D. C. Heath, 1987.

Solo, P. *From Protest to Policy: Beyond the Freeze to Common Security.* Boston: Ballinger Press, 1988.

Somerville, J. "Nuclear omnicide." Reprint from the *Churchman* August/September 1979.

————. "Nuclear 'war' is omnicide." Reprint from *Peace Research: A Canadian Journal of Peace Studies* 14 (1): April 1982.

Toch, H. *Violent Men.* Chicago: Aldine, 1969.

Wijkman, A., and Timberlake, L. *Natural Disaster: Acts of God or Acts of Man?* London/Washington, DC: International Institute for Environment and Development, 1984.

Yudkin, M. "When kids think the unthinkable." *Psychology Today* April 1984.

Name Index

Subject Index

abuse, 119, 120; of children, 45, 78, 119, 121, 122; and physical discipline, 121, 122, 124, 125

Accuracy in Academia, 136

adolescent identity crisis, 35–39

aggression, 5, 7–11, 47, 92, 117, 119; gender differences in, 120, 121; and parenting, 124–25; and sex-role stereotypes, 7–9; socially approved, 122

aggressive acts, 119

aggressive instinct (drive), 3–5, 8–13, 30, 125

aggressiveness, 3, 7, 11, 14, 48, 64

aggressive posture, 78

alienation, 22, 31, 35, 39, 51, 77

ambivalence, 64, 70

annihilation, 15, 18, 21, 30, 31, 35, 69, 70

anomie, 77

anxiety, nuclear, 27, 28, 31, 38, 41, 42, 46, 54, 71, 76, 88, 90, 95, 99–100, 104, 124, 135n

apathy, 26, 29, 39, 55, 58, 69, 76, 86, 99, 101, 104

apocalyptic dreams, 41, 42, 61, 66, 86, 93, 132n

apocalyptic promises, 31

arms production, 11, 13, 14

arms race, 11, 12, 14, 19, 22, 100, 101, 133n

atomic weapons (bombs), 18, 103, 110, 124. *See also* nuclear weapons

attitudes toward nature (conquest or cooperation), 21–23

attitudes toward nuclear war, 52, 53–67, 99; aged-based differences in, 84; of Americans, 56–63, 85–88; anti-nuclear, 53–58, 63, 64, 66, 84, 91, 132n; cross-cultural differences in, 81–95; of French, 83, 91–95, 134n; gender-based differences in, 85, 91, 92; of Germans, 82–91, 133n, 134n; pro-nuclear, 56, 57, 62–64, 84, 92, 132n; of youth, 39–43

burnout, 115

capitalism, 90

capital punishment, 122

change, 100, 101, 106, 110, 122, 125; in relationships, 122–123

Chernobyl, 101

child-rearing, 9, 10, 92, 120, 121

ABOUT THE AUTHORS

LISL MARBURG GOODMAN, author of *Death and the Creative Life*, received a Ph.D. in psychology from the New School for Social Research in New York City. Until her retirement in 1987 she was Associate Professor of psychology at Jersey City State College and concurrently held a position of senior clinical psychologist at a Psychiatric Services Center in White Plains, New York. Dr. Goodman has published articles on personality research and thanatology in scientific journals, and has made scholarly contributions at major psychological conventions and congresses in the United States, Canada, and Europe. The ramifications of life in the nuclear age has been her special interest since 1982 and she is now devoting her full time to research and writing on that subject.

LEE ANN HOFF, a nurse-anthropologist and crisis specialist, is Associate Professor of Nursing at Northeastern University, Boston. She is the author of *People in Crisis* and *Battered Women as Survivors*. Dr. Hoff teaches and does research on violence and suicide, women's health, and sociocultural aspects of health. She is active in developing a peace studies program at Northeastern, has founded the Life Crisis Institute, and is a frequent presenter at national and international conferences.